West Indian in the West

West Indian in the West

Self-Representations in an Immigrant Community

Percy C. Hintzen

NEW YORK UNIVERSITY PRESS
New York and London

NEW YORK UNIVERSITY PRESS
New York and London

Library of Congress Cataloging-in-Publication Data
Hintzen, Percy C.
West Indian in the West : self-representations in an immigrant
community / Percy C. Hintzen.
p.   cm.
Includes bibliographical references and index.
ISBN 0-8147-3599-1 (acid-free paper)
ISBN 0-8147-3600-9 (pbk. : acid-free paper)
1. West Indian Americans—California—San francisco Bay Area—
Ethnic identity. 2. West Indian Americans—California—San
francisco Bay Area—Social conditions. 3. Immigrants—California
—San francisco Bay Area—Social conditions. 4. San Francisco Bay
Area (Calif.)—Ethnic relations. 5. San Francisco Bay Area (Calif.)
—Social conditions.   I. Title.
F869.S39 W545 2001
305.896'972907307946—dc21   2001003120

Manufactured in the United States of America

10 9 8 7 6 5 4 3 2 1

To My Wife Joan Hintzen
For Her Dedication and Support

Contents

Acknowledgments

I am enormously grateful to those West Indian immigrants who agreed to share with me and my student researchers the details of their lives and insights into their understanding of who they are. These immigrants were not merely "respondents" but were also enthusiastic supporters of the project. I cannot thank them enough, and I hope that none is disappointed with its results. I hope, too, that I have answered many of their questions about their presence in the United States, as a small compensation for their valuable contribution to the book.

The book has benefited from the commitment and support of many student researchers, both graduate and undergraduate, at the University of California at Berkeley. In particular, I am deeply indebted to Allyson Nigorizawa, who came to the research project at a critical juncture and literally took over its administration when I was pressured with other duties. Allyson's constant encouragement and her persistent and insistent cajoling ensured that my focus remained on the task of research and writing. When she left the project, she recruited Imelda Walavalkar, who brought to it the same diligence, thoroughness, and enthusiasm. Allyson and Imelda took part in much of the data collection and project organization, and they also periodically cleaned up and reorganized my office to make the research and writing more efficient and manageable. This book is a testament to their help.

As graduate student researchers, Paul Dottin and Nathaniel Silva worked on different phases of the project, and both made tremendous contributions to its eventual outcome. Grace Chang, another graduate student, also provided assistance with the research.

Graduate students Claudia May, Cheryl Roberts, Anjelina Villafane, and Joan Hintzen and undergraduates Tala Dowlatshahi, Manijeh Fata, Raha Jorjani, and Lemlem Rijio did yeoman service as student interviewers. Their efforts are evident throughout the book.

I had the good fortune of working with Wendy Ledger, an excellent and diligent transcriber. I was always amazed at the speed and accuracy of her transcripts.

The project was supported by a grant from the Ford Foundation for departmental development, provided while I was chair of African American studies at Berkeley. I was one of the fortunate beneficiaries of the funding allocated to faculty research. The Office of the Dean of Social Sciences gave me a six-year stipend for department chairs, much of which supported the research for this book.

Frances Carter was my department's office manager while I was doing my writing and research. Without her stewardship, nothing would have been accomplished. Department staff Byron Spicer, Glenn Robertson, and Stephanie Jackson contributed to the smooth and efficient running of African American studies while I was preoccupied with research and writing and teaching.

The idea for this project came from work by Aurora Noguera-Devers, who wrote her senior thesis on West Indians in the San Francisco Bay Area. It raised interesting questions that I have attempted to answer in the book. Her work underscores the sophistication of today's undergraduates.

Finally, I would like to thank Jennifer Hammer at New York University Press for her patience, suggestions for reorganization, and support.

West Indian in the West

Introduction

This book emerged from my interest in identity construction among West Indian immigrants in the San Francisco Bay Area. At one level, it is an examination of how the understanding of identity and the way it is produced and reproduced explain the relationship between black West Indians and African Americans. Important in this regard is how the United States' racial construction intersects with West Indian immigrants' distinctive cultural baggage and resources (such as education and income). It is at these intersections that their notions of difference from African Americans are produced. Identity construction is related to patterns of affinity and antipathy, which are the particular foci of this study. In sum, my purpose is to explore the different and complex meanings of "West Indianness."

My choice of the San Francisco Bay Area was based on the patterns of identity construction and resource availability that differ from the typical West Indian communities in the eastern seaboard cities of the United States. In the Bay Area, West Indian identity is constructed around reference schemata of achievement and foreignness by a group that is disproportionately middle and upper middle class.

I consider authenticity to be the most important issue in the social sciences and one that should be the preeminent concern of scholars presenting and representing social reality. Do the data and their interpretation fully represent the collective and individual understandings of those being studied? Until now, social scientists have been able to avoid answering this question by falling back on notions of abstraction and interpretation. They make claims of "seeing" and "understanding" that are unfathomable to those whom they study. These social scientists' insights derive from special qualities of knowing unavailable to their "subjects." Not surprisingly, their conclusions cannot be confirmed except by other social scientists.

The issue of whose "understanding" is authentic and how to judge such authenticity has been a preoccupation of social science methodology. The many discussions of this subject need not be reproduced here in their detail. Those social scientists who subscribe to a more formalized view of social science "objectivity" and to notions of "value neutrality" distinguish between the "validity" of representations of social reality, presented as "data," and their "reliability." The demands of each are considered to be in conflict. The test of reliability pertains to the ability of social analysts to reproduce, independently, the findings of others, which demands prior agreement about the nature of social reality and how it should be measured. This test leads to conceptualizations and categorizations that emerge in intellectual debates among scholars that can have absolutely nothing to do with the way people understand their social world, broadly defined, which in turn leads to the argument for validity. This argument requires methodologies of induction in which, in a process of conceptualization, data gathered from social observations are abstracted and organized into "concepts" and their categories. In this process, the researcher's understandings and interpretation are paramount.

Anthropologists make similar distinctions between "-etic" and "-emic" approaches to observation and measurement. In the "-etic" approach, it is the researcher who decides how social reality is organized. Data are collected primarily for categorization and classification in order to differentiate societies and social systems. The "-emic" approach accepts at face value the representations and practices of the "subjects," as well as interpretation by the researcher, who may be assisted by informants and "opinion leaders." For those concerned with "authenticity," the "emic" approach is certainly more desirable, but it still raises a number of issues. The first is selectivity. The researcher continues to select the aspects of behavior to be observed, interrogated, presented, and represented. The second issue relates to contamination. That is, in their social interactions, "subjects" and informants attach meaning to their relationship with the researcher, assessing the consequences of his or her attitudes and behavior for themselves and their communities. Accordingly, they adapt their behavior to their understanding of the researcher's interests.

This book is the result of my own attempt to grapple with the issue of authenticity, which arose with particular force in an encounter I had with a potential "respondent" while conducting research in the West Indies. My project—still not completed—is an examination of the political economy and political sociology of the English-speaking West Indies. The self-described "sufferer" asked me about my interest in him, and I explained that the purpose of my research was to analyze conditions of poverty and powerlessness. Our conversation was as follows:

"You are a professor at an American university, and you live in America. You could never understand poverty and powerlessness in the West Indies."

"Of course, I could. I was born in the West Indies and lived here until my twenties. I have involved myself in the affairs of my country. And I am quite familiar with conditions of poverty from the experiences of both my own family and the family of my wife."

"But you and your wife are rich Americans. You can never know about poverty and powerlessness in the West Indies."

"I am neither 'rich' nor 'American.' I am West Indian."

"You may not be rich in America, but you are rich here. And here in the West Indies, you are American. You may be West Indian in America but not here."

"So according to you, I could never study poverty and powerlessness in the West Indies?"

"No, never. You have to feel it. You have to experience it. You could never tell people about me and my life, no matter how hard you try and what 'roots' you claim to have. All you will do is use me for your own benefit, to make money and get fame."

"So what would you suggest I do? What should I study?"

"Study yourself, people like yourself. You know them. You can't know me. You can never know sufferers."

This conversation occurred during a period of personal introspection. I had begun to examine my own position in African American studies at Berkeley, in response to the hostility expressed by some African American university faculty to the presence of West Indians among their ranks. These attitudes seemed to be directed particularly toward West Indians in African American studies. The hostility had been exacerbated by efforts to redefine the discipline in ways that elevated the study of Africa and its entire diaspora. African Americans scholars were concerned that the change would dilute their initial focus on race in the United States, and they accused the West Indian faculty of being more concerned with issues of political economy and identity. These were understood to be more relevant to the study of the Caribbean and its West Indian diaspora.

I came to the conclusion that it might be impossible for me to understand the attitudes and feelings of the African American faculty. But I did have an understanding of the West Indian community in the San Francisco Bay Area that was visceral, intuitive, and subjective, derived from my own experience as a West Indian involved in the community and its affairs. I had become interested in the attitudes of members of this community toward African Americans. Perhaps it was the hubris of West Indians that was fueling African American resentment. So I decided to heed the advice of the Trinidadian "sufferer" and to study "myself."

I see this book as my own contribution to the methodological debate on authenticity. Because I am both its subject and its analyst, I do not need an "informed interpreter" and an "opinion leader." Furthermore, the study of a community by someone from the "inside" eliminates "contamination" of the data by a researcher who does not "belong." As a member of the community, I am in a position to "know" what is important and what to look for and to "understand" the meaning of what is being said and observed.

To a certain extent, therefore, I began this project already knowing its outcome. While there were vast differences in the participatory experiences of the respondents who were interviewed, my own Bay Area West Indianness afforded a considerable degree of empathy. I was able to understand by putting myself in the place of the respondents whom I studied. Their representations and practices "made sense" to me because they were constructed from the "matter-of-fact," "taken-for-granted" world in which I lived. This is what, I believe, gives the study its authenticity.

Identity is experienced, performed, and communicated in representations and practices that include memory, images, symbols, rituals, interpretations, and understandings and are what I observed and interpreted in this study of West Indians in the San Francisco Bay Area. These representations and practices all involve, to a greater or lesser degree, selected elements of the cultural baggage brought into the geosocial arena in which identities are produced and reproduced.

One of this study's fundamental assumptions is that people use their identities to ensure the most beneficial and desirable social positioning for themselves, both individually and collectively. They use collective understandings of difference in the particular social arena in which they participate for the social production of their own identities. People's social identities emerge from this accommodation to and contesta-

tion of the collective understandings of themselves as members of identific communities. Because these understandings exist in popular consciousness, they may differ in different geosocial arenas.

The social mechanisms for communicating identity are important, as
they require the organization and presentation of the reference schemata used in determining "who one is." In turn, "who one is" stands at
the core of the cognitive construction of identity, to which significance
and meaning are attached. Even though they are organized into a single
identific community, individuals construct their identities around their
own experiences. In their interpretation of these experiences, they combine different elements of the reference schemata around which their
collective identity is organized. This process gives rise to considerable
differences in self-representations and practices among individuals
within a collectively identified group. For this reason, I pay particular
attention to the relationship between individual life history and identity construction.

The methods I used to collect my data derive from the understandings of West Indian identity in the American collective conscience.
These are the understandings to which West Indians respond in the social construction of their identity. Various elements of these understandings are emphasized in different geosocial arenas in the social
construction of identity, leading to differences in the ways that identity
is understood, represented, and practiced. This is what I mean by the
contextual basis of identity.

This study examines the ways in which West Indians publicize their
collective presence in different geosocial locations. The rituals and symbols around which these public displays are organized communicate the
meaning of their collective presence. My analysis presents data from carnivals, sport events, clubs, restaurants, associations, and other arenas
publicizing identity. A collective identity represents a response to the
geosocial arena in which it is organized, produced, and reproduced. Thus
I compare public festivities in New York with those in the San Francisco
Bay Area to emphasize the contextualized nature of identity construction
in general and of West Indian identity in particular. The social geography
of New York produces a social identity of West Indianness that is different from that of California and shows how location shapes the ways in
which identities are organized and understood.

To construct an identity, a community must be objectified and reified,
as well as confirmed and reasserted. Private and semipublic ritualized

social gatherings serve these functions, as members of the community use them to engage in ritualized performances of identity. These performances offer boundary-defining mechanisms and exclusive displays of membership and belonging. And they provide an opportunity to articulate the reference schemata of identity construction. I examine these boundary-defining rituals and identific performances for what they say about the social composition of the West Indian community in the San Francisco Bay Area. Like public rituals, they also communicate the meanings that members attach to their presence in a particular geosocial location.

Public, semipublic, and private rituals and performances are important for two other reasons. First, they are used to form popular understandings of difference by the display of images in popular conceptualizations of the group. These are presented in symbolic and ritualized displays. Second, a community uses rituals and performances to claim a legitimate presence in a particular geosocial location. They communicate information about the presence of members of that community. West Indians use exotic images that exist in popular consciousness to announce their presence in a particular geosocial location. These performances also communicate to a popular audience their understandings of "who-one-is." For West Indians in the San Francisco Bay Area, these images revolve around notions of success and achievement, two of the defining principles of their identity.

Identity is constructed at both the collective and the individual level. At the individual level, people select different elements from the reference schemata of identity construction to form their own self-representations and practices. Their selection is based on their particular life history. To form a collective identity, people chose from the community's core values in a process of interpretation, reinterpretation, and reorganization.

How did I select my respondents, maintain their anonymity, and protect their confidentiality? I gathered data through participants observations, oral histories, and informal interviews with members of the West Indian communities in both New York and the San Francisco Bay Area. I made sure that my respondents in the Bay Area represented the community's islands of origin, economic and educational backgrounds, and age groups. All were over eighteen years of age and were chosen from a list obtained through a snowballing method.

My access to West Indians was facilitated by my strong personal connection to the West Indian community and my active role in its affairs. Accordingly, I took the names of West Indians from the West Indian community and its professional organizations, social clubs, sports organizations, friendship networks, West Indian–owned businesses, and other groups to which I personally had access. I then asked these persons and organizations for references to other persons and other organizations, and I used these contacts to compile a master list of West Indians organized according to country of origin, income, professional status, sex, and education. I selected the final group of forty-five persons, who were contacted by phone and told about the nature and purpose of the project. Once they had given their verbal consent to be interviewed, a graduate research assistant arranged with them a time and place for the interview. Before the interview, all the respondents were given an informed-consent document to read and sign.

This procedure ensured that no information about any potential respondent would be made available to anyone other than myself until I obtained his or her initial verbal consent. Second, it gave the respondent three chances to decide whether to participate. The first was at the time of my initial contact. The second was when the research assistant contacted the respondent. And the third was when I requested a signed consent.

Student researchers conducted all the interviews, at the respondents' residence, place of employment, or another agreed-upon location. The interviews were conducted in private, usually but not exclusively where no one else was present. Some of the respondents requested that others, usually family members, be present, and we agreed.

The purpose of the interviews was to gather and record the respondents' life histories. The student interviewer focused on those social, cultural, economic, and other background factors that helped form individual social identities. Some of their questions elicited recollections of the historical "memories" that helped construct their identity. Each interview usually lasted around ninety minutes and was recorded. When necessary, a follow-up interview was requested. Someone also transcribed the audio recording of each session. I then analyzed the respondents' life histories as "texts."

A study of this sort has many advantages, including the following:

1. Its contribution to understanding identity formation by individuals in societies organized around notions of race.

2. Its contribution to understanding identity construction by immigrants adapting to their host community.
3. Its contribution to knowledge about West Indian immigrants to the San Francisco Bay Area. Until now, most of the research on West Indian immigrants has concentrated on populations that settled along the eastern seaboard of the United States.

I took great care to protect the respondents' confidentiality and anonymity, with the exception of one case study already in the public record. I changed the names of the respondents and omitted their countries of origin from any textual reference. I also changed the details of their occupations and, in some instances, their qualifications. When possible, I described their backgrounds in general terms, without an effort at camouflage. Most West Indians came to California via New York; fewer came via Great Britain. A significant minority came to attend universities throughout the United States. These details were included in the case histories because they apply to many in the San Francisco Bay Area. All references to illegality in the individual case studies were omitted. Because I chose the case studies as being representative, the stories they tell are shared by many in the West Indian community. While the respondents will recognize themselves in the following pages, I am confident that they will not be recognized by others.

1

Identity, Arena, and Performance
West Indians in San Francisco Bay

The West Indian immigrant community in the San Francisco Bay Area of Northern California differs in important respects from the larger West Indian immigrant communities on the East Coast of North America. It is relatively small, numbering fewer than ten thousand. There also is no spatial community of West Indians. Rather, most immigrants are spread out throughout the Bay Area with the majority in San Francisco and Alameda Counties, in the East Bay, in the peninsula counties, and in the city of San Jose. At the core of the community are persons who came from elsewhere in the West Indian diaspora rather than directly from the West Indies. Most of them relocated to the Bay Area because they were offered jobs there or were transferred to the area by their employers. Many are military personnel or professional or skilled workers. Others came as students to one of the Bay Area's colleges or universities. To this core were added dependents, nondependent family, and those who immigrated because of friendship ties. In socioeconomic terms, many of the immigrants are middle to upper-middle class. The chapter focuses on West Indian identifying rituals, concentrating on the participants' class, their small number, and the absence of a spatial community. It examines the sites of these ritualistic performance of identity in order to relate the arena of the performance and the performance rituals themselves to the community's cognitive constructs of "West Indianness."

The San Francisco Bay Area is a ten-county region that stretches more than 160 miles from north to south and 40 to 50 miles from east to west at its widest point. The 1990 U.S. Census listed the region's population at 6,253,311. This area contains some of the richest counties in the United States, with housing prices among the highest in the nation. It is also the location of numerous universities, colleges, and research institutions, including Stanford University, the University of

California at Berkeley, and the University of California at San Francisco. It is one of the most ethnically diverse regions in the United States and a prime location for immigrants, particularly those from Asia and Latin America.

In 1990, there were 9,019 persons living in the Bay Area who listed themselves as West Indian (excluding Hispanics) in their first or second response to the "ancestry" question on the U.S. Census (U.S. Bureau of Census 1991:CP-3-2). The total West Indian–born population in the United States is 727,191, and 842,101 persons are listed as having West Indian ancestry. New York City alone, it is estimated, contains around half a million "West Indians," and more and more are settling in Miami (U.S. Bureau of Census 1991:26–28).

West Indian Identity and the American Discourse of Difference

Along with some other immigrant communities, West Indians are popularly considered to be a "model minority." This term refers to meritocractic success, applying particularly to the American racial discourse. That is, different groups are thought to receive what they have earned and deserve (for a discussion of the model minority and its origins, see Fong 1989; Petersen 1971; Steinberg 1981; Yong-Jin 1994). Accordingly, West Indians are seen to have overcome obstacles of poverty and the disruption of immigration to achieve, on merit alone, middle and upper-middle-class socioeconomic status. Indeed, scholars like Thomas Sowell have used West Indians' putative success to refute arguments that African Americans' poverty is the result of racial discrimination:

> The West Indian success pattern likewise undermines the explanatory power of current white discrimination as a cause of current black poverty . . . [C]olor alone, or racism alone, is not a sufficient explanation of income disparities within the black population or between black and white populations. Even educational disparities do not account for the West Indian higher socioeconomic status, for in New York metropolitan area they have no educational advantage, in terms of years in school, over native blacks. (Sowell 1978:43)

Another explanation for West Indians' success, by sociologists Glazer and Moynihan, refers to their unique "cultural baggage." West

Indian culture, they argue, extols the virtues of hard work, savings, and investment:

> The West Indians' most striking difference from the Southern Negroes was their application to business, education, buying homes, and in general advancing themselves. . . . They average high in intelligence and efficiency, there is practically no illiteracy among them, and many have a sound English common school education. They are characteristically sober-minded and have something of a genius for business, differing almost totally, in these from the average rural Negro of the South. (Glazer and Moynihan 1963:35)

This view has been supported with reference to the supposed "overrepresentation" of West Indians among the successful black population of the United States. Sowell contends:

> West Indians have long been greatly overrepresented among prominent Negroes in the United States. From Marcus Garvey, James Weldon Johnson, and Claude McKay in an earlier era to Stokley Carmichael, Shirley Chisholm, Malcolm X, Kenneth Clark, James Farmer, Roy Innes, W. Arthur Lewis, Harry Belafonte, Sidney Poitier, and Godfrey Cambridge in more recent times. (Sowell 1978:41)

These claims made about West Indians' success are much more important for the part they play in the ideology of race relations than for what they say about the reality of the West Indian immigrant presence. They also are part of the reference schemata used to construct the West Indian identity in the United States.

Scholars such as Philip Kasinitz (1988), Kristin Butcher (1994), and Reynolds Farley and Walter Allen (1987), however, who have studied West Indian immigrants over the last two decades, have come to different conclusions about their supposed "success." Butcher (1994) found little difference in the employment rates, marriage rates, average weeks of work, and average wages of native-born African American men and West Indian male immigrants. Moreover, she found that African Americans who had moved across state boundaries were economically more successful than immigrant blacks, including West Indians. After taking into account their location of residence, family type, and education, Farley and Allen (1987) concluded that the income gap between African Americans and West Indians is quite small and that African Americans actually earn more than their West Indian counterparts. Furthermore, Dodoo

(1991) found that the returns from education were lower for West Indian immigrants than for African Americans:

> Evidence to the contrary notwithstanding, the myth of the model minority continues to persist in popular understandings of the West Indian migrant. This myth receives constant reinforcement both from within and outside the West Indian community. It is sustained by tendencies to present as universal examples of West Indian success those migrants and their descendants who have risen to positions of national prominence.

Most West Indians live in New York City, and most are employed in the service sector. For this majority, there is a disjuncture between the generalized socioeconomic achievement of its members and the myth of the model minority. That is, their typically low income and occupational status hardly qualify them for inclusion in a "model minority." For them, the contradiction between socioeconomic status and the popular understanding of achievement is resolved by redefining their own West Indian identity. In doing so, West Indians in New York emphasize other elements in the reference schemata of identity formation. Studies have shown that the children of low-skilled West Indian immigrant workers are more likely to be identified as African American (Waters 1994). But this is not the case for foreign-born immigrants, who overwhelmingly differentiate themselves from African Americans. While their offspring may acknowledge their West Indian background, most of them regard themselves as African American, as they see little advantage to a West Indian identity (Waters 1994).

This does not mean that a West Indian identity is unimportant. For the West Indian lower class, however, the meaning of "West Indianness" differs significantly from the popular conception of West Indian success. That is, as one of the city's ethnic communities, West Indians use their identity to secure service-sector jobs or resources. (This evidence is based on personal observations and a continuous familiarity with New York City's West Indian community between 1973 and 1979, on a semicontinuous basis as a frequent visitor to New York since 1979, on the observation of family and friends living in New York City, and on discussions with informed observers of the West Indian community.) West Indians dependent on New York's service sectors are most likely to live in Brooklyn, and also Queens and the Bronx. Brooklyn serves as the primary location for the majority of

West Indian–owned commercial and retail businesses and service providers, including professional ones, to the community. Because they cater to West Indian tastes in food, clothing, music, and the like, their locations have become public sites for the display of West Indian ethnicized identity.

West Indians use the public spaces in those sections of Brooklyn where they predominate to demonstrate their presence and to make claims of belonging in the city and in the United States at large. In other words, they have created identifiable "West Indian" communities in New York for symbolic displays of their identity. However, neither the sites, symbols, nor rituals of West Indianness in New York lend themselves to self-representation as a model minority. There is nothing particularly "affluent" about New York's West Indian physical communities; their working-class socioeconomic status precludes displays of success and affluence.

The West Indian identity is located in the ethnicized construction of difference that is typical of New York City. West Indians have become one of the city's myriad ethnic communities with, probably, no more or no less significance attached to their identity as West Indians than that attached to the identity of members of any of New York's other ethnic communities. They participate in the symbolic discourse of ethnicity in the same ways that other ethnically identified groups do. Their rituals of kinship, country, friendship, and associational ties are probably much more significant to self-representation and self-understandings of "who one is" than to "West Indianness" per se. There may be little interest in being West Indian apart from the opportunity it provides to claim a space in the city's ethnic organization and to protect and maintain privileged access to service-sector jobs.

West Indians in high socioeconomic-status positions do have available to them the prerequisites for displays of achievement consistent with their identification as a model minority. Successful black middle-class West Indians thus have a vested interest in symbolically separating themselves from the black-white dichotomy in the American discourse of racial difference, and they can do so in self-representations that incorporate elements of their status as a model minority. They can use their identity as immigrants and foreigners to escape from the stigma of being "African American." Such an identity may also insulate them from racial prejudice when they interact with whites. Their West

Indian identity may be an assertion of their socioeconomic status as equal to that of their white counterparts.

Ariana Hernandez-Reguant found a similar pattern of class-based "ethnicization" in the African American middle class (Hernandez-Reguant 2000). Middle-class African American rituals and symbolic displays in the ceremony of Kwanzaa mirror those of the West Indian middle class. Like the West Indian displays, they signal separation from the black-white dichotomy of a racialized America. The rituals of Kwanzaa and the symbolic representations conveyed in its images reflect values associated with white American middle-class morality. And these representations, argues Hernandez-Reguant, explain the general acceptance of Kwanzaa by mainstream society. The rituals also explain the position that Kwanzaa has attained alongside other ethnic celebrations. Hernandez-Reguant goes out of her way to emphasize the ethnic, rather than the racial, character of Kwanzaa, its rituals and symbols pertaining to ethnicized rather than racialized images of difference. Kwanzaa is one form of ritualistic representation employed by African Americans to symbolize their inclusion in the ethnic mosaic of America alongside other ethnic communities, including those of the European diaspora.

Data presented by Waters (1994) confirm the predisposition of middle-class West Indians toward an uncategorical embrace of West Indian identity. This tendency is handed down through generations. Unlike their urban working-class counterparts, the majority of suburban and college-bound teens that Waters interviewed represented themselves as West Indian. By claiming an immigrant status, they were able to maintain a distinction between themselves and African Americans. In other words, the connection between West Indian achievement and West Indian identity appears to be related to socioeconomic status. Waters found this connection especially with increased interaction with whites and residence in a desegregated neighborhood.

A study of West Indians in Los Angeles conducted by Joyce Justus (1983) provides additional evidence of the association among West Indian identity, notions of immigrant foreignness, and socioeconomic status. At the time of the study, the majority of recent West Indian immigrants to Los Angeles were professional or technical workers. The blue-collar workers were employed predominantly in semiskilled occupations. West Indians did not live exclusively in spatially or geographically defined communities. Rather, Justus found a "collective consciousness of West Indianness" among these immigrants "which finds expression in a multiplicity of Caribbean organizations." She also found class exclusiveness, with lower-class West Indians being "often rebuffed in their attempts to make social contacts and associate themselves with the middle class." Among the immigrants, Justus discovered many of the traits associated with a model minority status, as well as efforts to distinguish themselves from African Americans (Justus 1983: 131, 132, 142–43).

Cursory evidence from an unsystematic survey of West Indians in the San Francisco Bay Area conducted in 1991 (Noguera-Devers 1991) suggests that their socioeconomic profile is quite similar to that of West Indians in Los Angeles. Despite the difficulties of reliability posed by the "snowballing" method of selecting respondents for the survey (it excluded potential respondents not normally associated with other West Indians), the study does offer a picture of the community's composition. Of those interviewed, 49 percent held professional or technical jobs, 11 percent held clerical jobs, and 25 percent held service-sector jobs. The second two categories contained a large number of students, 36.4 percent, many of whom were employed in the service and clerical sectors. These figures suggest that in the aggregate, the occupational status of West Indians in the San Francisco Bay Area was higher than that of both whites and African Americans there. This fact was reflected in the educational attainment of the West Indians interviewed: 94 percent had graduated from high school, and 85.1 percent had had some college experience. The median family income of the West Indians interviewed was $22,188, which was higher than that for African American families ($16,025) but less than that for white families ($26,376) (Noguera-Devers 1991:10–12). Note that the West Indians' income was skewed downward by the large number of low-earning students among the respondents.

Images of Immigrants in California

On July 1, 1996, there were around 8 million foreign-born residents in the state of California's total population of 32.4 million. This amounted to 33 percent of all foreign-born residents residing in the United States and 25 percent of California residents. Because of their numbers, immigrants and their families are quite visible. At the same time, the images and understandings of immigrants held by mainstream Californians are not uniform in regard to cognitive constructs containing notions of worth, desirability, and merit. Such understandings of immigrants vary according to their particular countries and regions of origin. The familiar image of the "illegal" pertains primarily to Mexican and, to a lesser degree, Latino migrants, particularly those from Central America. The popular media and politicians speak of Mexicans and Latinos as posing a threat to the nation's integrity and as making illicit and illegal claims on state resources. A common theme is the cost to the "taxpayer" of providing services to these illegals and their children and also that Latinos "take jobs" away from legal residents. During the 1980s and 1990s, these historically constructed representations fueled the escalating anti-immigrant sentiment and culminated in the passage of California Proposition 187 in 1992 which was aimed at prohibiting access by illegal immigrants to state-provided services, including education and health care.

Undocumented California migrants and their documented counterparts from Mexico and Central America tend to be clustered in the labor-intensive sectors of the economy, particularly in agriculture, the textile and garment industries, construction, and the service sector, especially "care" services. Thus, their socioeconomic and occupational profiles resemble those of West Indian immigrants on the East Coast. But whereas the historically constructed images of the "undesirable" migrants in California pertain almost exclusively to Chicanos/Latinos, West Indian immigrants are not conceptualized in these terms. Hence, a space is created for alternative understandings of their presence and role in California's political economy.

✳Understandings of Asian and Pacific Rim (excluding Latin American) immigrants are formed from cognitive constructs of the "model minority." These constructs are confirmed by the visibility of highly educated and wealthy immigrants from East Asia (particularly Korea, Hong Kong, and Taiwan) and, more recently, from South Asia. These immigrants took advantage of the Immigration and Nationality Act of 1965, which reversed the practice of excluding Asians from the United States. Asian immigration between 1965 and 1980 increased by 1041.5 percent (U.S. Immigration and Naturalization Service 1984:table 2). It is in the context of the popular images of these immigrants that the West Indian identity was formed in Northern California.

West Indian Immigrants to California

✗The historical construction of difference in California made available to West Indian immigrants three possible "locations" for the construction of their self-representation and identity. Their blackness provided a location in the racialized space of the African American. Their "foreignness" offered a location in two cognitively constructed spaces. The first was the one occupied by the "undesirable" group of Mexican and Latino migrants in the popular imagination, and the second was the space of the "model minority" occupied by Asian immigrants. Several factors combined to place West Indians in the cognitive space occupied by Asian immigrants.✗

The first factor was the preexisting generalized representation of West Indians as a "model minority." This, perhaps more than anything else, explains the pervasiveness of West Indians' images of success in whites' consciousness, despite the occupational parallels between Latino migrants on the West Coast and the majority of West Indians in New York City.

The second factor is the history of socioeconomic achievement among West Indian immigrants to California. This has to do with "pull factors" of West Indian immigration to the West Coast that worked against the unskilled and low skilled and favored the qualified and educated. The overwhelming presence of Mexican, Latino, and Pacific Rim migrants in the labor-intensive and service sectors of the California economy has succeeded in shutting out unskilled and low-skilled West Indians. At the same time, those in the West Indian middle class are well suited to exploit opportunities for the skilled and educated in California's economy, by using their racial identity to gain access to the "affirmative action" positions available to the African American population. West Indians also have been able to exploit the political strength of the African American community in Los Angeles and the San Francisco Bay Area. The formidable influence of black politicians grew out of the massive political mobilization during the Civil Rights movement of the 1960s and 1970s. Black leaders were able to win support from the progressive white community and, particularly, from the Chicano and Latino communities. Their political organization and support helped propel African American politicians into the mayorships of Los Angeles, Oakland, Berkeley, and San Francisco. Indeed, in the 1980s and 1990s, Willie Brown, an African American state representative from San Francisco, held the state's third most powerful position, that of speaker of the Assembly. African American political power also allowed Tom Bradley, the black mayor of Los

Angeles, to mount a credible campaign for governor by winning the De-
mocratic nomination in 1982 (see Dymally 1972; Fisher 1992; Horne
1995; Sonenshein 1993; Wyman 1987).

Black political clout in California was accompanied by access to
public- and private-sector resources that opened opportunities to African Americans throughout the state, particularly in its cities. The black
West Indian middle class was able to enter this "racial space" created
by African American political power, as reflected in the growth of the
West Indian population in Los Angeles from around 500 before 1950
to around 50,000 by the early 1990s (Justus 1983:131).

West Indian Immigrants to the Bay Area

Images of Bacchus versus the Model Minority

The subjective performance of West Indians' identity in the San
Francisco Bay Area has been complicated by their geographic dispersion and the absence of a central geographic space where their symbols
of identity can be displayed and rituals performed. Members of the
community therefore have had to make a conscious effort at self-representation by organizing and participating in identific rituals and by
constructing symbols of West Indian identity in numerous decentralized locations. Although they necessarily differ, all efforts at self-representation use the popularized symbols and images of the West Indian
cultural forms making up the cognitive schemata of "West Indianness"
shared by Americans, particularly white Americans. As semiotic indices, these symbols and images are readily recognized as the "boundary markers" of West Indianness. As such, they indicate the character
and nature of the West Indian community. These symbols and images
include music, dance, "spicy" food, and a "carnival" spirit that serve
as reference schemata in the cognitive construction of a cavalier, fun-
loving, bacchanalian, accommodating character.

These "boundary markers" combine in subjective performances
with a second complex of ritual performances that serve as indicators
of merit, achievement, and worth in self-representations as a model minority. These two sets of references to West Indianness are contradictory representations of the nature and character of the West Indian.
That is, the rituals of boundary demarcation use symbols of bacchana-

lia, whereas the rituals of the model minority use symbols of achievement, purposefulness, hard work, and family values.

The two sets of symbols and rituals are connected in the construction of the West Indian identity, although they serve fundamentally different functions. The subjective performances defining boundaries are critical to distinguishing West Indians from African Americans. This symbolic separation from the black-white dichotomy is complicated, however, by the strategic importance of a "black" identity for the upward mobility of West Indians and their access to economic and educational opportunities. But this dilemma is resolved by confining subjective performances and self-representations as a model minority to private and semiprivate spaces and locations from which African Americans are largely excluded. Collective rituals of identity performance and displays of self-representation take place in the public arena only as part of collective displays involving other immigrant communities. Very rarely are they exclusively West Indian events. Rituals of self-representation as a model minority tend to be performed in spaces away from the African American community and away from the arenas where "blackness" counts.

The private or semiprivate dispersed locations of West Indian ritual performances, however, militate against the construction of West Indians as a political community. Because West Indians are not organized as a community with a distinctive political presence, they are free, as individuals, to activate their racial identity as blacks and to identify with the causes of the black community. They can rely on the political, organizational, and strategic resources of the black community to protect their rights against discrimination and prejudice. They also are free to participate in the African American networks organized to provide strategic support to its members. The self-representation as blacks is important to West Indians in the San Francisco Bay Area as a means of protecting their rights and furthering their interests, but it also muddies their relations with African Americans.

Symbols, Rituals, and Subjective Performances

Boundary-Defining Rituals

At the most general level, music, food, and dance symbolize the West Indian identity. Reggae, calypso, soca, and zouk are the representative musical forms, and the steel band is the representative musical instrument. They all serve as semiotic indicators of the region and its diaspora. In the San Francisco Bay Area they signify the West Indian presence and character.

West Indian musical forms are popular among broad segments of the population in the San Francisco Bay Area. Reggae, in particular, is routinely played on a few of the more youth-oriented radio stations. Public and some commercial radio stations have allocated slots to West Indian music, and several West Indian bands in the area are hired by nightclubs and booked to play at private and corporate parties and gatherings. Other than West Indians, white Americans seem to provide the bulk of the audience and clientele for these local bands, especially the steel bands, most of which are made up of predominantly or exclusively white musicians. Performances by local bands are complemented by visits from a constant stream of internationally famous West Indian musical groups, which attract huge audiences. The annual Reggae Festival held in San Francisco, for example, is attended mostly by young whites. The popularity of West Indian music in the San Francisco Bay Area has much to do with the white desire for the exotic and has contributed to the creation of a legitimate space for Caribbean culture in the area. Notions of "foreignness" and "exoticism" lend themselves to the white embrace of West Indian cultural forms and help locate West Indians outside the boundaries of American race relations and ameliorate or suspend the effects of rules of aversion that govern black-white relations.

But the white embrace of West Indians is not an embrace of equals. Rather, it is the embrace of the exotic. Accordingly, in their boundary-defining rituals of demarcation, the West Indian community is forced into performances and symbolic displays emphasizing its exotic character. This is evident in the use of food to signify identity.

Clubs and Restaurants

Ethnic restaurants provide places to publicize identity and are central to the process of exoticization. This is the case for West Indian restaurants in the San Francisco Bay Area. Over the past twenty years, many such restaurants have opened and closed in San Francisco, Oakland, and Berkeley. Their dishes and menus are organized into symbolic manifestations of the exotic images linked to popular understandings of West Indians. Typical dishes are West Indian staples such as curried goat, peas and rice, rotis, Jamaican patties, plantains, and stewed fish. Beverages include "ginger beer," "sorrel," and "mauby." The dishes and beverages are not allowed, however, to "stand on their own" in symbolic communication, despite their "natural" and obvious association with the West Indies. Rather, the restaurants use their menus to highlight their exotic offerings. Descriptions of the dishes use generalized popular, exotic images of the West Indies, and sometimes the dishes themselves are given new and exotic names. One West Indian restaurant in Berkeley, named "Caribbean Spice," follows this pattern. On its menu, standard West Indian dishes have been given new names evocative of white society's popular and exotic images of the West Indies. Examples are dishes with names like "Reggae Chicken and Sexy Rice," "Hotter Than Hell Pepper Pot," "Lambada Fried Fish," and "Crazy Goat," evoking images of the dance, sex, heat, and wild abandon associated with West Indians and the West Indies. Beverages are served in glass jars, contributing to an image of primitive naturalness. A similar primitivism is reflected in the "jungle" decor of the restaurant. Everything points to the accommodation of and accessibility to its white clientele. For example, a concocted drink called "ginpin" (a combination of ginger beer and pineapple) was highlighted in Caribbean Spice's beverage selections. The owner explained that the pineapple was added to counteract the spiciness of the ginger in order to appeal more to "white" tastes. This predisposition toward accommodation and accessibility is typical. West Indian patrons are routinely told that the amount of spices and peppers has been reduced in the preparation of the dishes so as to make them more palatable to white tastes.

This evocation of images of dance, sex, heat, normlessness (i.e., craziness), nature, and welcoming accommodation reflect the northern industrialized world's popular conception of the West Indies. These images occupy the semiotic center in the publicization of the West Indian presence and in the reification of its character and predispositions.

Food, music, and dance combine in a semiotic cacophony in all the semipublic locations of West Indian identific performance. But restaurants are much more than sites for the publicization of what is foreign, exotic, and different about West Indians. Together with West Indian clubs (in 1997 only two clubs were identified as West Indian), they serve as semipublic arenas where West Indians in the San Francisco Bay Area engage in ritualized self-representations and performances of their identity, where the West Indian community socializes publicly. In this regard, they serve as surrogates for residential ethnic communities.

West Indian clubs and some of the restaurants go out of their way to present themselves as cultural centers. For instance, one club offers dance and exercise classes (to the accompaniment of West Indian, Brazilian, and African music) during the day. Some clubs and restaurants intersperse their evening activities with cultural entertainment and an occasional fashion show. Most host performances by various West Indian and Brazilian carnival costume bands that participate in the annual San Francisco Carnaval held annually on Memorial Day weekend. One of the restaurants serves as the location of a "Mas Camp" where one of the West Indian carnival bands is headquartered. It is the place where the costumes are made and displayed, the band's activities are organized, and meetings and fund-raising events are held.

These boundary-defining mechanisms are used by the West Indian community in the Bay Area to display their self-definition and are organized around informal rules of access that underscore the community's sense of "difference" and foreignness. These rules highlight differences between West Indians and African Americans through practices of exclusion and emphasize notions of foreignness through practices of inclusion and celebration of Africans, Asians, Latinos, and Pacific Islanders. And they use the presence of whites to demonstrate the West Indians' separation from America's racial discourse of difference and their own, West Indian, sense of accommodation and inclusiveness.

The clubs and restaurants in the Bay Area are locations not merely for the performance of West Indian identity; they also serve to position West Indians among the group of "Third World" immigrants. Reggae music is played because of its popularity among whites, Chicanos, Latinos, Asians, and Pacific Islanders. There is less emphasis on other types of West Indian music such as calypso, soca, and zouk. The clubs play African and Latin music as well, to attract a diverse group of patrons— except for members of the African American community.

The rituals and performances demarcating identity are carried out with the use of separation and exclusion directed at members of the African American community, particularly when the West Indian identity is publicly thematized. None of the clubs plays any African American music (as opposed to traditional African), despite the popularity of rap among West Indian youths, and rhythm and blues and jazz among the older generation of West Indians. The owners of one of the clubs explained that African American music tends to attract "the wrong crowd." They claimed that the club was African American before they took it over, and they wanted to avoid the problems with drugs and violence associated with its former clientele (interviews with the club's owners, 1996).

West Indians generally expect African Americans to be excluded from their semipublic arenas of performance. In fact, when the African American presence becomes obvious and significant, West Indian participation noticeably declines. In the late 1980s, African American youths attracted to reggae began to attend the Caribbee, one of two West Indian clubs operating at the time. The Caribbee was located in Oakland, a city with a large population of African Americans, and soon its West Indian clientele began to complain. The older West Indians stopped coming altogether, declaring that the club had gone "downhill." They then began to patronize the second of the West Indian clubs, located in an upscale, white, peninsula community across the Bay, because of its unstated policy of African American exclusion. They claimed that the move made them feel "safe," that this club preserved and protected the "family environment" that typified West Indian social spaces.

In their publicized performances of identity, West Indians signify their distinctiveness through a symbolic use of "exotic" boundary-defining images that reinforce their difference from African Americans. At the same time, they emphasize the accommodation and inclusiveness of other racial and ethnic groups, thus locating West Indians in the community of "foreigners" and signaling their accommodation of whiteness.

The San Francisco Carnaval

The most publicized display of West Indian identity can be found at the San Francisco Carnaval, held annually on the Sunday of Memorial Day weekend. The Carnaval is not perceived as an exclusively West Indian event but as one shared by various exoticized communities, with Brazilians and Caribbeans occupying pride of place. The San Francisco Carnaval provides an opportunity for the West Indian community to demonstrate publicly its boundary-defining exotic character, its immigrant status, and its accommodation of multiculturalism. It is a performance directed at a predominantly white audience, with an emphasis on dance, music, food, and elaborate costume bands, some featuring scantily clad women and men, conveying the image of an exotic Caribbean. Carnaval is also a means through which the West Indian community presents itself as a foreign presence in the San Francisco Bay Area. There is little to attract members of the African American community, and the absence of its members is noticeable. The event is discussed in detail in the next chapter.

The Oakland Carijama

West Indians also use public festivities to advertise the uniqueness of their cultural identity and to create a "psychic" return to their homeland (see Manning 1990:35; Nettleford 1988:197; Nurse 1999:674–77). Such festivities are used to reinforce their sense of community. The most public thematization of a distinctive and exclusive West Indian identity in the Bay Area is an annual event called Carijama, organized on Memorial Day, the day after the San Francisco Carnaval festivities end. It is held in Oakland and draws a crowd of around 5,000, primarily from the West Indian community. The primary audience for the event is the West Indians who participate in the San Francisco Carnaval. The displays play up the exotic in costumes, music, dances, and food. But the intention of its organizers is to create a more "Caribbean mood." In the words of one of the Carijama's organizers, it is "much more spontaneous and go with the flow," reflecting the popular understandings of West Indianness (interview with Jacquie Artman, 1996). The event is an "exclusive" one that reifies the existence of a Caribbean community for its members. This role is confirmed by one of its organizers: "I just look at it as we are all one Caribbean people, the same people, from the same region, coming together."

Open-House Events

The West Indian community is reified most frequently at open-house events, publicized through invitation, word of mouth, or some form of public announcement. These events include public dances, large parties, or "pot luck" affairs. Guests may be asked to pay an entrance fee or some kind of monetary contribution. They are even more inner directed as rituals of reification and self-reinforcement through which the West Indian community reproduces itself. Their focus is almost exclusively on music, food, and dancing, although occasionally they include cultural presentations in the form of displays of Carnaval costumes or West Indian dance. Events like these are the most exclusive display of West Indian identity.

Clubs and Associations

Because of their restricted membership, clubs and associations are located in the interstice between public and private. As semiprivate entities with public visibility, they are ideal vehicles for the public thematization of socioeconomic status. Furthermore, their exclusivity allows considerable control over terms and conditions of entry, and so there is little evidence of the exoticized symbolic displays in the more public arenas. Perhaps the most important of these associations and clubs in the San Francisco Bay Area are the Jamaican Association and some of the soccer and cricket clubs. Occasionally, other country-specific associations are formed and operate for a time and then disappear. Two such attempts were a Trinidad and Tobago association and a Guyanese association, both of which soon folded. In 1993 the African, Caribbean, and American Network International was created as an overarching cultural and social organization and a chamber of commerce for the West Indian community, with some African participation. Its agenda was to establish a "West Indian town" like the Chinatowns in major American cities. But like its other country-specific counterparts, this organization functioned for a while and then disappeared.

The Jamaican Association of Northern California has been the most successful of the country-specific organizations. It was established in 1975 and is still operating. Although active membership is reserved for Jamaican immigrants and their descendants, associate membership is open to all West Indians in the Bay Area. The association's core members are successful professionals, and the association's events are formal affairs usually aimed at raising funds. It is an ideal forum for the demonstration of West Indian success, with an emphasis on achievement signaled in numerous ways, including a "scholarship fund" that awards grants to high school and college students of Jamaican descent.

Cricket matches are another venue for the West Indian thematization of difference and the ritualized performances of identity. Indeed, playing the game of cricket on an American playground is in itself a symbol of refined difference. Its casual formality and slow-paced refinement are contrasted with the characteristic fast pace, physicality, and aggressiveness of American sports. The cricket teams are generally mixed, with most of the players from one of the cricket-playing countries of the British Commonwealth. There are two predominantly West Indian teams in the San Francisco Bay Area, which also have players from India, New Zealand, and Australia. Unlike the San Francisco Carnaval, cricket provides an arena for the display and performance of West Indian achievement, success, and morality. Many of the team players are well-to-do, and quite a few are university graduates. The game thus offers an opportunity to display symbols of success, such as the cars driven by team members and their families, their clothes and jewelry, the "country club" atmosphere of lawn chairs and umbrellas, and the toys brought to entertain the children.

The ritual of the cricket match serves as a demonstration of the inclusiveness of the West Indian community and its distance from American racial categorizes. It is a multiracial and multicultural event that includes both West Indians and non–West Indians, but it is not open to all. Rather, the match is an exhibition of the unity produced by the commonality of foreignness, in which whites and nonwhites from overseas display their success in America and as a way of identifying with British, Australian, New Zealand, and South Asian immigrants who are either white or successful.

The family plays a central role in West Indian self-representations as a model minority. Therefore, through their emphasis on the family, West Indians try to project a morality and ethic that is different from the popular (i.e., white) conception of African American family life as chaotic and unstructured. West Indians also try to show the moral superiority of their background through images of the family. Accordingly, they bring their families and friends to the matches, which continue beyond the actual game itself at the home of one of the team members, also an arena for the further display of a stable and intact family life.

Besides their function as a display of foreignness, achievement, and success, cricket matches are decidedly West Indian events. The food is typically West Indian and is prepared for the team by the players' families. West Indian music is played, and West Indian beer (usually Jamaican Red Stripe or Guinness stout—the favorites of West Indian males) and rum are the alcoholic beverages of choice.

University Groups

Many of the ritual performances and symbolic representations of West Indianness in the Bay Area are displays of educational achievement, as exemplified by university groups. These groups also serve to preserve the distinction between West Indian and African American students. The Bay Area's universities are ideal places for ritualized displays of worth, achievement, and merit. The West Indian students at Stanford University and the University of California at Berkeley have organized student groups for West Indians only. Sometimes their meetings are informal, with the students getting together in one another's apartments or homes where West Indian food is served. Usually the meetings are attended by West Indian professors, who occasionally host them. At other times, the students organize more formal groups that meet to hear papers on West Indian topics by both themselves and faculty. They also invite West Indian faculty from throughout the Bay Area to informal events in order to "network."

West Indian students usually avoid African American student organizations and do not participate in African American–oriented campus events, thus communicating a West Indian identity and locating West Indian students with those whose presence in higher education is based on merit. This message is important at the Bay Area's universities, given the collective understanding of West Indians as successful and high achievers. In their self-representations as West Indians, these students try to insulate themselves from stereotypical images of African Americans as unintellectual and undeserving of a place in higher education. Many even retain or assume the distinctive West Indian accent in order to signify their identity and emphasize their West Indian background in class discussions and conversations with professors. These rituals of identity identify them as educational achievers and separate them from the educational underachievement and affirmative action preference attached to African American students in white imagination.

The West Indian students at the Bay Area universities have various conceptualizations of their identity. Those from other regions of the United States may see themselves as different from the West Indians in the San Francisco Bay Area. Some may have identities based on self-understandings as ethnicized West Indian Americans, as is typical of the large West Indian communities on the East Coast. Others may come with a well-developed African American identity. Once enrolled in one of the Bay Area colleges, however, these students quickly embrace a West Indian identity for the benefit it offers in higher education, that is, the separation from American blackness afforded by a West Indian identity.

House Parties

Most ritualized performances of West Indian identity in the San Francisco Bay Area take place at private gatherings in the home and are the primary means of communicating a model minority status. Whereas the stereotypical symbols of the West Indies evoke the "Carnival spirit," the opposite is true in performances in which a model minority status (the themes of order, formality, family, organization, success, preparation, and hard work) is displayed. West Indian self-representation as a model minority is confined largely to the homes of those who have achieved visible success. West Indians of low socioeconomic status are usually not invited to these events and can be made to feel quite uncomfortable if they attend, for their presence cannot be accommodated in self-representations of success and achievement.

The ethnic composition of the guests at these events can vary considerably. Invited non–West Indian coworkers, neighbors and friends of both the hosts and guests provide an outside audience for these ritual displays and performances. The presence of guests from diverse racial and ethnic backgrounds underscores the openness and accommodating nature of the West Indian character and confirm West Indian success to the West Indian community and a non–West Indian audience.

The home is an ideal site for the display of education, occupation, achievement, and income (i.e., through the display of material possessions). Guests are usually introduced to one another with information about their jobs and education, although their casual and informal nature masks their symbolic significance in the West Indian's self-representation.

Celebrations and rites of passage are occasions for ritualistic displays of success. Birthdays, anniversaries, christenings, graduations, and baby showers are ideal opportunities for the public acknowledgment, through speeches, of the accomplishments of both hosts and guests. Less formal gatherings are held to celebrate public holidays such as Christmas, New Year's Day, Thanksgiving, Labor Day, and Memorial Day, as they offer only a limited opportunity for the formal accounting of the successes of hosts and guests.

Spouses, parents, and, when appropriate, children participate in the symbolic celebration of the family at both the private and less private, formal and less formal events. Except at the more formal evening gatherings, children are always present. Sometimes their activities are separate from the adults', but at other times, they join in each other's activities, particularly dancing or formal presentations and announcements.

Private (as opposed to open-house) parties are held in the evenings and usually begin with a cocktail gathering after which a buffet meal is served. Speeches and ceremony follow. They end after an extensive period of dancing in a space designated for that purpose. Small clusters of people gather in other rooms of the house, chatting and consuming beverages. There is a certain degree of status (usually occupational) segregation in these clusters. The larger the gathering is, the more segregation there is, and it is much more pronounced at public events such as large parties, dances, night clubs, and even Carnaval. This tendency toward class exclusiveness signifies the social positioning within the West Indian community itself.

Ambiguity and Conflict in Identity Construction

Persons of West Indian descent have various reasons, which are not necessarily obvious, for wanting to establish an identifiable space for themselves in American society. At certain times and under certain circumstances, West Indians reject their West Indianness and identify themselves as African American. At other times, though, they may feel caught between the pulls of both communities.

Soccer

The conflicting pulls of identity are particularly strong for younger and less successful West Indian males. In the San Francisco Bay Area, soccer matches are perfect arenas to display an ambiguous identity. Unlike cricket, soccer does not have as much ritualized formality. The game's physicality and fast pace closely resemble the typically American games of baseball, basketball, and football. There is little emphasis on family participation, and most of the spectators are male. Thus, playing soccer can signal location in the interstice between a West Indian and an American identity. The young and less successful West Indians to whom soccer appeals usually also are attracted to African American popular culture, particularly music and dress, especially when their low socioeconomic status may prevent them from participating in rituals of achievement and success.

Despite its ambiguity, soccer does provide an arena for self-representation as a West Indian. There are a number of West Indian soccer teams in the Bay Area, and the makeup of their members—Latin American and African—signals their "Third World" character. Some teams have a few English players as well. Every year, a "Caricom Tournament" is held, in which teams representing the various islands of the region play against one another. (The Caribbean Community—or Caricom, as it is known—is the group of English-speaking Caribbean countries that have established a formal organization for the purpose of economic integration and coordination.) The tournament is an all-day family affair featuring West Indian music and West Indian food.

At the same time, however, self-representations of West Indian identity through the game of soccer lack the symbols and displays of achievement and success consistent with a model minority status. Successful West Indians do not attend soccer matches, perhaps because of the game's ambiguity and its parallel displays, in structure and location, of stereotypical and racist African American images. Moreover, the game is played very aggressively, with constant bickering and verbal skirmishes among the team members, and the West Indian teams are located in Oakland, a city strongly identified with the African American community.

The contrasts between soccer and cricket are clear. Cricket is formal, nonphysical, leisurely, not contentious, and foreign, and it offers an ideal opportunity for the display of family unity. Cricket games are played exclusively in the affluent suburbs, and there are no teams in Oakland. Thus, the cricket match combines symbols of difference, foreignness, and model minority status in West Indian self-representations. Soccer, in contrast, provides a site for asserting a West Indian identity devoid of images of success, offering young people a symbolic means of embracing what is American and, particularly, what is African American, without having to reject their West Indian identity.

The Military and Marriage

Veterans' attempts to bridge the divide between the West Indian and African American communities underscore the centrality of the notion of difference from African Americans in the West Indian identity construction in the San Francisco Bay Area. Over the years, a small number of West Indian immigrants, primarily males, have been stationed at one of the many military bases in and around the Bay Area. Some joined the military during the Vietnam War for the opportunity to obtain legal resident status and eventually citizenship. Others saw in the military a secure job with good benefits and opportunities. A number of these West Indian veterans settled in the San Francisco Bay Area, and some have been quite active in West Indian community affairs.

The military, however, offers few opportunities for self-representation as West Indian, and so many West Indian enlistees embrace African American culture and identity. This is the point made by a West Indian veteran living in San Francisco:

> So I was in the military in-depth in American society. As a matter of fact, it was to the point where I had sort of almost escaped being a [West Indian], I was so embedded in American culture, black American culture, which is when I really—I had a chance to learn about and be around and just absorb. (interview with West Indian veteran)

This embrace of an African American identity by West Indian military personnel is reflected in dating patterns and the selection of marriage partners. Many marry African American women while in the service. But when they leave, the path back to the West Indian community for these veterans may be difficult, even though they have acquired many of the trappings of success and achievement. Most use their veterans' benefits to buy their own homes and use their skills and military service to get access to skilled occupations and/or higher education. They become typical West Indians through their incomes, occupational status, and home ownership.

The veterans' continuing ties to the African American community complicate their self-representation as West Indian. Some maintain their ties through their spouses. In one instance, to manage the conflicting pulls of the two communities, a small group of veterans formed an informal clique within the West Indian community, and their African American wives developed a strong bond among themselves. These bonds facilitated the veterans' involvement with the West Indian community while supporting one another as African Americans. The veterans and their African American spouses hosted events that incorporated rituals and symbolic representations of both communities, such as parties to watch sports events like the Super Bowl, parties to celebrate birthdays, barbecues, and special holidays such as Christmas and Easter, in other words, occasions recognized by both communities.

For the most part, the veterans' African American wives seemed to get along well with one another. But their relations with West Indians were often tense, sometimes forcing their husbands to make a choice. In every instance when one of these marriages ended in divorce, the West Indian divorcee chose a West Indian as his new partner. One of the veterans even went back to the West Indies immediately after separating from his wife, met a woman from his island, became engaged, and married her as soon as his divorce became final. Another separated from his American wife to begin a relationship with a West Indian woman, opened a business that catered to West Indians, and became one of the organizers of a West Indian carnival band participating in the San Francisco Carnaval. A third decided to return to the Caribbean. Most of the veterans who remained married to African Americans eventually disappeared from the arenas of West Indian collective self-representation. A few were able to negotiate their West Indian identity while remaining married to African Americans, particularly when their African American spouses had become integrated into the West Indian community. Many of the latter even severed their connections with African Americans.

Conclusion

Identity is contextual, emerging in the social space where hegemonically imposed understandings and their contestations intersect with existing cultural, social, economic, and political realities. It is conditioned by the resources and understandings of those who are collectively identified.

Persons from the English-speaking Caribbean who live in the San Francisco Bay Area choose a West Indian identity because of its popular association with the myth of the model minority. But the choice is complicated by the need also to identify as "black" in order to gain access to resources needed for upward mobility. By identifying themselves as black, West Indians in the United States can legally claim resources reserved for the African American community. In this way, they can protect and enhance their socioeconomic interests by making common political cause with the African American community. At the same time, however, they need to establish and maintain their differences from African Americans, which fuel their assertion of a West Indian identity.

West Indians in the San Francisco Bay Area exploit exoticized images of difference to distinguish themselves in the American racial discourse. Symbolic displays and performances are essential to creating a West Indian space in the social mosaic of the San Francisco Bay Area. At the same time, West Indians assert their status as a model minority in their rituals of self-representations, through symbolic displays of studiousness, intellectualism, success, hard work, material possessions, and commitment to family. The contradictions between the exoticized images of West Indian difference and the images of success and achievement associated with a model minority status are managed through the practice of separation.

2

Performance and Meaning in West Indian Immigrant Identity
Public Displays of Self-Representation

Identity is partly communicated through rituals of self-representation. It derives its meaning and emerges from the social space where the representations and practices of those being identified become intertwined with understandings imposed by the host community. Social identities are the responses to these understandings. They are conditioned by the culture and common participatory experiences of those who are being collectively identified. On the one hand, they incorporate those aspects of popular understandings that shape the collective consciousness about the group. But on the other hand, they emerge as challenges and signal the rejection of popular conceptualizations. Social identities are framed by the particular social, cultural, economic, and political arena to which the community and its members (individually or collectively) are responding. In other words, they impose meaning on self-representations and identifying practices, whose contexts are continuously changing. In sum, identity is determined at neither a collective nor an individual level and neither in time nor over time. The identific community and the individuals within it are constantly refashioning their identities and the way in which they are represented as they move from one social arena to another. This is part of the process of negotiation to achieve the best social positioning against the limitations imposed by popular conceptualizations of "who one is."

This chapter focuses on collective self-representations of West Indian identity in the United States, by examining the public ritual of carnival performed by immigrants from the English-speaking Caribbean who live in New York and the San Francisco Bay Area. I argue that these collective self-representations are responses to the social, economic, political, and cultural contexts of the locations in which the carnival is performed. The carnival provides an opportunity to negotiate and publicize identity on many levels. One level is the relationship between West Indians and African Americans, on which it is, first, a response to the black-white dichotomy of racial discourse running throughout collective representations and practices in the United States. Second, it is a means of establishing and communicating the political location of the West Indian community and of negotiating and publicizing the community's relationship with the dominant white mainstream. And third, it is a negotiation and publicization of the West Indian community's position within the broader category of immigrants. I look at three of the ritual performances of carnival, in San Francisco, San Jose and Santa Clara Counties in the San Francisco Bay Area, and Brooklyn in New York. (In New York the event is called Carnival, as it is in Trinidad, whereas in San Francisco, it is called Carnaval, as it is in Brazil; and in Santa Clara it is deemed a "music and cultural festival," even though it incorporates features of Carnaval.) I believe that these locations represent different social and political arenas to which the construction of the West Indian identity must respond.

At the most elemental level, rituals of West Indian identity reflect the exoticized images of "West Indianness" contained in Americans' (particularly white Americans') cognitive schemata. These images convey understandings of a cavalier, fun-loving, bacchanalian, accommodating character. As semiotic indices, they are universally recognized and thus may be considered the "boundary markers" of the character and nature of the West Indian community. They are conveyed in West Indian music, dance, "spicy" food, and a "carnival" spirit. The public festival of carnival provides a perfect venue for publicizing these collective images in the self-constructions of West Indian identity. This phenomenon is "diasporic," since it is not central to the West Indian collective identity at home. That is, it derives its meaning as an expression of West Indian collective identity only among immigrant communities abroad (see Manning 1990; Nurse 1999). As a ritual in the West Indies, carnival is historically and characteristically Trinidadian, with calypso music, soca performance bands, and theme-based masquerade bands dominating the performance. Indeed, it was only its vast potential for attracting tourists that led to the recent introduction of carnival in other English-speaking West Indian countries, for the carnivals in the West Indian diasporas of New York, Toronto, and Notting Hill in England predated their introduction to most of the West Indies.

Carnival became a collective self-representation of West Indian identity in the United States because it coincided with Americans' popular consciousness. For West Indians, this consciousness serves as a basis of differentiation from African Americans, as it locates the West Indian community outside the black-white dichotomy of American racial discourse. This dichotomy is at the root of *generalized* attitudes of aversion held by whites toward African Americans, reinforcing among whites a ritualized distance from African Americans. Indeed, because whites have embraced elements of West Indian identity in the American popular consciousness, they exempt West Indians from the aversion that governs black-white relations. Accordingly, boundary-defining rituals such as carnival stand at the center of the West Indian ethnicization or the development of notions of permanent foreignness that can alter and even suspend the terms of black-white relations in racialized arenas of interaction (Hintzen 1999). The white embrace of West Indians is not one of equals, however, but an embrace of the exotic. Thus in their boundary-defining rituals, the West Indian community is forced into exoticized performances and symbolic displays, as is evident in the performance of carnival.

Another, more favorable understanding of West Indians held by the American mainstream comes out of their collective identification as a group of permanent foreigners. Like other immigrant communities, West Indians have come to be considered in popular understandings as a "model minority," exhibiting the ideals of success associated with the white mainstream achieved through merit, sacrifice, and hard work. In popular discourse, West Indians are regarded as having overcome the obstacles of poverty and migratory disruption to achieve, on merit alone, middle- and upper-middle-class socioeconomic status.

Together, the images of the West Indian as exotic and a model minority define the boundaries within which West Indian identity is negotiated in the United States. They combine differently in different contexts, and they are used differently in West Indians' efforts to negotiate their locations in their particular social arenas. New York City, San Francisco, and Santa Clara present fundamentally different challenges for identity construction, each demanding different strategies for collective self-representation. In all three locations, the West Indian carnival is the principal public arena in which these understandings are performed, communicated, and contested.

The Brooklyn Carnival

The areas of West Indian commerce in Brooklyn have become public sites for the display and performance of a particularly New York version of West Indian identity. By confirming their presence and claiming a space in the city and in the United States at large, West Indians in New York create a "West Indian" ethnic community.

One way to signal and demonstrate a community's political, social, and cultural presence and significance is through ethnically centered parades and festivals, which are related to the development of a "public ethnic memory" (see Saverino 1996). Public displays involving parades and festivals have become the principal mechanisms employed by ethnic immigrant minorities to define their collective selves. In this way, they can shape the collective consciousness of themselves and define and determine their role and significance in the community.

In New York, the identific and the political combine when each community signals its political, social, cultural, and economic influence through public displays of its collective presence—which often are parades. Some of the more important are the Chinese New Year parade in Manhattan, various St. Patrick's Day parades held in different boroughs, a Greek Independence Day parade, various Puerto Rican Day parades, a Cuban Day parade, a Cinco de Mayo/Comite Civico Mexicano parade, a Salute to Israel parade, a Philippine Independence Day parade, and a Columbus Day parade. More recent immigrant communities quickly learn to make known their presence through similar collective public displays. The South Asian community has its Shri Lakshmi Narayan Mandir "Holi" parade in Queens, and Pakistani Americans, their Independence Day parade in Manhattan.

Philip Kasinitz's authoritative book (1992) on West Indians in New York devotes an entire chapter to the annual Labor Day carnival, pointing out the tensions that it causes. He concludes that the carnival is an "ethnic statement" asserting the "massive presence" of West Indians in New York and their "cultural particularity" to the outside world. It is aimed at "group mobilization" (Kasinitz 1992:148). This is an important statement given the diversity of the West Indian community and the national factionalism, inherited from the region, that creates serious and fractious divisions. At the same time, the carnival is a strategic political demonstration devoid of political statement or position, as is commonly the case with the Irish and Puerto Rican parades (p. 134). Indeed, the "politics" of carnival has little to do with the promotion of West Indian politicians or the community's political positions. Rather, the carnival is a demonstration to those in power that they should take the community seriously as a political, social, and cultural bloc.

There is absolutely no doubt about the Labor Day carnival's success in this regard. It is, unquestionably, the largest street festival in the entire United States. By the late 1990s, the parade was drawing more than 2 million people, with some estimates placing the number at more than 3 million. It has become the principal mechanism for publicizing the Crown Heights section of Brooklyn, where it is held, as the social and cultural center of West Indian America and certainly of West Indian New York. The parade has also become a statement of claim to a piece of New York turf, which the community seized from the city's Hasidic Jews. The battle over turf between the two communities continues to create tensions and crises, usually with the carnival parade as a backdrop. In 1994, when Labor Day coincided with Rosh Hashanah, the Hasidic community was left powerless to stop what appeared to them to be a sacrilege. Carnival revelers, feeding the American imagination with exoticized bacchanalia, danced their way past the headquarters of the Lubavitcher Hasidic movement as the latter tried to celebrate one of its holiest days (see Noel 1994a; Sengupta and Pierre-Pierre 1998). Jewish leaders used their considerable political clout to attempt to stop the parade and, failing that, to have it rerouted around their headquarters. Calling the carnival "another Rwanda" in the making, the leaders demanded that those areas of Crown Heights where Hasidic families lived be placed off limits and that the festivities end by sundown. The conflict got the attention of the top politicians in the state and city, including the governor and the mayor. The West Indian community prevailed in the negotiations after agreeing to make some concessions, which included the establishment of a buffer zone around the Jewish headquarters and a commitment to end the festivities at 6.00 P.M. (Noel 1994b). The latter was honored only in the breach.

The political significance of the West Indian community is demonstrated in its massive presence at the Labor Day parade, underscoring to politicians running for state and city office the need to pay particular attention to it. It was during the 1980s that the carnival began to acquire political significance. In 1984, Marty Markowitz, the white representative from Crown Heights to the New York State Senate, was selected as the parade's grand marshal. His selection was viewed as an endorsement of him by the West Indian community and as a slap in the face of the African American political establishment. It was also, though unintentionally, a symbol of the community's independence from African American political culture and sensibilities. Thus the selection of Markowitz highlighted the broader ethnocultural distinctions between these two communities. Jesse Jackson, who spoke at the parade, unwittingly emphasized this distinctiveness by making a political speech geared exclusively to the African American community, thereby failing even to acknowledge that the event was West Indian. Nor did he acknowledge the political and sociocultural leaders of the West Indian community before introducing the African American politicians—to whom the parade organizers directed their fury for "stage managing" Jackson's appearance (see Kasinitz 1992:154–56).

Despite the organizers' efforts to neutralize the event, politicians began to use the carnival to demonstrate their political commitment to the community. By the end of the decade, unable to stop them, the event's organizers decided to invite and welcome all politicians to participate, in this way emphasizing the parade's political neutrality (Kasinitz 1992:157–58).

The politicians' increasing interest in the community, as shown in their attendance at the Labor Day festivities, was sparked by the tremendous growth in New York's West Indian population. Much of this growth came in the wake of the immigration reforms passed by Congress and signed into law in 1965. The new legislation enabled increases in the number of people immigrating legally from Caribbean microstates. Kasinitz (1992) points out that in the ten years after the reforms, the number of persons immigrating legally from the West Indies surpassed the total number for the entire seventy years before the act went into effect. And the numbers continue to rise, fed by the opportunity to sponsor immediate family members.

Many of these new immigrants moved to New York. Between 1982 and 1989, the New York Department of Planning reported that a total of 153,000 people from twenty-three Caribbean countries had moved into the city (Purdy 1994). By 1990, U.S. Census figures placed the West Indian population in New York–Northeastern New Jersey–Long Island at 502,051 for those who gave West Indian ancestry as their first response, and at an additional 25,658 for those who gave it as their second response (U.S. Bureau of Census 1991:CP-3-2). And the numbers continued to grow over the next decade. It is not surprising, then, that in the 1990s, the West Indian carnival was drawing "state and local politicians by the dozens" (Purdy 1994). Attendance at a preparade breakfast became mandatory for politicians seeking state or city office and for those representing districts with large concentrations of West Indians. In 1994, State Senator Markowitz remarked on the growing recognition by these politicians that the West Indian community was "one of the most important political forces in the city" (see Purdy 1994).

The community's growing political influence brings with it a growing share of public resources, for the carnival allows elected politicians to show the community that its needs are being met. Indeed, the New York carnival is supported by public funds from several agencies, including the Office of the Mayor, the city's Department of Cultural Affairs, the New York State Council on the Arts, the Brooklyn Borough president, the Brooklyn Museum, and the Brooklyn Botanical Garden. The mayor also hosts a reception at the official residence in honor of the event (see Office of the Mayor of New York 1997).

The organizers and participants recognize the carnival's political significance as a demonstration of the social and cultural presence of West Indians in the city. A Jamaican-born councilwoman for Brooklyn was one among many pushing to give the carnival a more political edge. "When you look at the numbers of people," she declared in the politically charged atmosphere of 1994, "you can see a potential to become a serious economic and political force to be reckoned with." She went on to fix the goal that each of the sixty musical and dance groups participating in the 1994 parade register twenty-five people to vote (Purdy 1994). Despite the organizers' commitment to political neutrality, there has been a small but perceptible increase in the parade's political content. In 1994, many New York West Indians voiced dissatisfaction with the organizers' decision to make concessions to the Hasidic Jewish community over the issue of Rosh Hashanah. The popular opinion was that the community should not have given in to the demand that the parade end at six. Tensions were already running high between West Indians and the Hasidic Jewish community. In 1991, a Hasidic driver of a car killed a seven-year-old West Indian boy in an accident. Afterward, the West Indian community erupted in four days of violence, culminating in the stabbing death of a Hasidic man. The incident and its aftermath became flash points in an ongoing ethnopolitical struggle between the two communities. That year, Hasidic Jews began to prepare a petition to stop the parade, but as testament to the political power of the West Indian community, the effort was abandoned. "There was a time," observed State Senator Marty Markowitz in 1994, "when there was Italy, Ireland and Israel for New York City. Now you have to add on the Caribbean as a major power center" (Purdy 1994:1).

The parade has also been used as a symbolic venue for efforts at conciliation. Mayor David Dinkins, who was the grand marshal in 1991, invited half a dozen Hasidic rabbis to march with him. One of the rabbis then used the parade as an opportunity to call for "brotherhood, camaraderie, friendship and peace"(Purdy 1991). But this did little to quell the growing tensions over political, social, and geographic turf.

Unlike the more intentionally political Puerto Rican Day and Columbus Day parades, the West Indian carnival has attempted to avoid politicization. Nonetheless, it occasionally has been used to indicate the community's position on particularly volatile issues. For instance, in 1997 the carnival provided a forum for many in the West Indian community to condemn the police torture of Haitian immigrant Abner Louima. Their protests were directed at the mayor for his defense of the police's behavior in the incident. While there was no organized or sustained political protest, many of those at the parade used the mayor's presence to express the community's discontent, through boos, catcalls, and the display of political banners. The parade's organizers also allowed Louima's attorneys to march alongside the black mayoral candidate Al Sharpton, one of Louima's most vocal supporters. The enthusiastic reception that Sharpton received left no doubt where the community's political sentiments rested (Fan, Finnegan, and Siegel 1997). In 1998, the parade provided another opportunity to voice discontent with the mayor. This time, the issue was the repressive manner in which he dealt with participants in the Million Youth March in Harlem (Gonzalez and Breen 1998).

Notwithstanding these protests, the carnival is not a political event. It delivers no systematic political message nor is it an expression of the community's collective political sentiments. Rather, the parade's emphasis is on the social, cultural, and performative. It is a celebratory festival, and the general consensus is that nothing should detract from this. Many people see politics as an unwelcome intrusion in an event that "should be about singing and dancing" and having a good time (Fan, Finnegan, and Siegel 1997). But a few decry what they see as a wasted opportunity for political organization. Colin Moore, a Guyanese attorney, politician, and columnist, has expressed considerable disappointment in the parade's apolitical emphasis, blaming the parade's organizers, whom he considers stuck in "parochial roots . . . unable to impose discipline, organization and creativity necessary to transform the Carnival into a significant political event" (Moore 1985:15).

Along with the politicians has come big business, using its association with the carnival to advertise and solicit the community's patronage. Major corporations, including AT&T, American Airlines, Con Edison, Chase Manhattan Bank, Citibank. NYNEX, Pepsi-Cola, Time-Warner, and Western Union have rushed in to provide sponsorship in recognition of the West Indian community's economic prosperity. Equal in their enthusiasm are the news media which, in addition to broadcasting and reporting the event, are among its major sponsors (Office of the Mayor of New York 1997). The parade has also become a big money earner for the city; in 1992, the parade generated an estimated $70 million in additional revenues.

The history of the West Indian carnival in New York parallels that of the West Indian community itself, mirroring the role and influence of West Indians in New York City's politics, culture, and community. The carnival started as a nostalgic celebration by a Trinidadian in 1928 in the hall of an apartment house in Harlem. In the 1930s, this evolved into a singing and entertainment show featuring a few masqueraders and calypsonians at a club in Greenwich Village. The organizer, a Trinidadian bandleader, also hosted ancillary shows and dances in Harlem and on the Upper West Side. In 1942, the big Harlem dance was moved to Manhattan, where it began to attract Trinidadians and other West Indians from throughout the city who were familiar with this pre-Lenten tradition. The first street event was held in the 1930s in Harlem, and the annual parade began after World War II. This was the first effort to model the event after Trinidad's carnival, with its masquerade bands and accompanying steel or string orchestras. The first accommodation to North America was made in 1947. Because of the weather, the small but growing annual event was shifted from the days immediately preceding Lent to Labor Day. But this was a concession not merely to the weather but to its integration into the American holiday tradition. With the move to the streets, carnival became identified with the entire West Indian community. Although the permit for the street event in Harlem was suspended in 1964 because of violent incidents, the tradition had been set. One of the Trinidadian organizers of the Harlem event then formed the United West Indian Day Development Association and revived the carnival festivities with a small, though illegal, street parade near his apartment. In 1969 official permission was granted for the parade to be held at its current venue on Eastern Parkway in Crown Heights. The change was initiated by the new leaders of the now-named West Indian American Day Carnival Association (see Hill 1994; Kasinitz 1992:140–43; Nunlely and Bettleheim 1988).

Carnival emerged from the longings of nostalgic Trinidadians for the pre-Lenten festivities of their homeland. With calypso and steel bands central to its performance, it was able to attract other immigrants from the Anglophone Caribbean, most of whom recognized that calypso and the steel band were the region's signature musical forms. The exceptions were the immigrants from Jamaica, who nonetheless quickly embraced carnival as an expression of their West Indian identity.

Collective forms and expressions of pan–West Indian identity are largely absent in day-to-day and face-to-face activities and in the social networks of members of the West Indian community. Instead, affinities and associations are, for the most part, island specific. Thus the carnival provides an opportunity for people to come together in a symbolic display of a collective ethos manufactured from the demands of the New York milieu. In their everyday lives, these people see their disaporic identities as rooted in their specific countries of origin. Such country-specific identities do not disappear on Labor Day but are reflected in patterns of participation at the carnival festivities that publicize national rather than regional identity. On the day of the parade, a profusion of flags represents the various countries, and designated sections on the parade route have become country-specific gathering places.

It is not the carnival's specific patterns of behavior that symbolize the West Indian identity but the totality of its symbolic display, the cognitive constructions of the West Indian "essence" in the popular imagination of mainstream America. Calypso, steel bands, open sexuality, percussive music, a fantasy world represented in masquerade bands, an emphasis on fun and enjoyment, alcohol, and exotic food all combine to create an image of the exotic West Indian in ways that no other expressive form from the region can do.

Carnival is also an exclusively black representation of the Anglophone West Indian presence in New York. Other racial and ethnic Caribbean representations are conspicuously absent, particularly the 150,000 to 250,000 Indo-Caribbeans living in the city. They come mostly from

Guyana, and Trinidad and Tobago where they comprise more than 50 percent and 42 percent, respectively, of the two countries' populations. The absence of Indo-Caribbeans can be attributed to their different pattern of racialization and ethnicization in the United States, unlike that of Afro-Caribbeans, who have become identified with the African diasporic presence because of their shared history with the African American descendants of slaves. Conversely, the Indo-Caribbean community has become involved in an alternative discourse of belonging, that of the Asian immigrant, and emphasize this distinction even in their choice of residence. Indo-Caribbeans gravitate to the Richmond Hill and Jamaica districts of the New York borough of Queens. From these ethnic enclaves, they have formed an identific alliance with the Asian-Indian immigrant community to which the West Indian carnival is not relevant. Of the more than 2 million participants in the carnival, Indo-Caribbeans are estimated to account for no more than 500 to 1,000. Instead, they use the city's India Day parade as the public expression of their ethnic presence. Their choice to identify with Asian Indians has made them almost invisible as a distinct community. Unlike Afro-West Indians, they are not considered a separate ethnic group by the U.S. Census, and they complain of being overlooked by the New York business community despite their relatively large numbers (see Strozier 1997).

As an expression of the Anglophone Afro-West Indies, the Brooklyn carnival also excludes Hispanic, Francophone, and Dutch Caribbean representations in its symbolic displays. Recently, the carnival's organizers have tried to include the Haitian community in the masquerade bands and other cultural and performative elements. The Haitian community's Afro-Caribbean exclusiveness and its presence in the same geographic areas as its English-speaking counterparts explain its ready accommodation by the carnival. Except for their different language, Haitians are identical to Anglophone Caribbeans in almost every respect.

Efforts to include other Caribbean communities have failed. In 1997, the organizers announced their intention to make the event "international" in celebration of carnival's thirtieth anniversary. They made plans to include "Latino, Jamaican, French Creole, and Indian Caribbean communities and cultures" and representations from "Brazil, Haiti, and other countries" (Office of the Mayor 1997). But despite these efforts and with the exception of the Haitians, the carnival remains exclusively a performance of collective identity by blacks from the Anglophone West Indies.

The San Francisco Carnaval

In their self-representations, black middle-class West Indians want to separate themselves symbolically from African Americans. Being designated as permanent foreigners, therefore, relieves them of the stigma of being "African American" and partly insulates them from white racial prejudice. The more they interact with whites, the more important their identity as West Indian becomes.

Unlike their unskilled counterparts, middle-class West Indians come with considerable advantages in regard to education and racial categorization. Furthermore, California's social culture allows them to distinguish between their racial identity and their cultural identity as immigrants. They are not considered "American" ethnic groups but foreigners who are popularly understood to be legitimate and desirable. In this respect, the ethnicization of immigrants in the Bay Area differs from that of New York, where legitimate claims of belonging rest on being transformed into ethnic Americans.

Identific displays by the Bay Area's West Indian immigrant community are complicated by their wide geographic dispersion. Unlike New York, San Francisco has no geographic community of West Indians that can facilitate and accommodate permanent displays of symbols and rituals of identity. There are no opportunities for a continuous performance of identific rituals, so ritual and symbolic displays must be held in decentralized locations.

In public arenas, music, dance, and food combine in identifying rituals and performances in different ways than they do in New York. The San Francisco Carnaval is at the center of these performances. It is held each year on the Sunday of Memorial Day weekend. Although it is not an exclusively West Indian event, it is also not all-inclusive as identific representations of the entire immigrant presence. Rather, it is a collective performance by exoticized immigrant communities with African influences and African roots, with Brazilians and Caribbeans occupying pride of place. Even though Carnaval is held in the Chicano district of San Francisco, there is not much evidence of Chicano participation. Rather it is the exotic Latino who is on display alongside those from the Caribbean. Carnaval provides the opportunity for these immigrant communities to demonstrate publicly their boundary-defining characters and immigrant foreignness. Unlike the New York festivities, Carnaval is not a racialized display but is targeted to a predominantly white audience. Part of its message is multiracial accommodation.

The San Francisco Carnaval began as an expression of the white embrace of the exotic, and in this, its origin differs significantly from that of its New York counterpart. A white American, Pam Minor, who in 1968 moved to the city from a rural town 120 miles away, was its first organizer. She was making masks, banners, and musical instruments when she decided to organize the event in 1978. Her role in creating Carnaval was not informed by knowledge of Caribbean cultures or of carnival traditions from other countries. Rather, her background was in American country music. (The following account draws heavily from a 1997 interview with Pam Minor.)

The first Carnaval was held in December 1978 as a small sidewalk parade, stemming from Minor's desire to create a new "tradition." But it was anything but new, becoming instead merely a replay of the pagan tradition of placating and honoring the gods when the "sun was furthest away from the earth" (Minor 1997). On December 21, participants wearing masks and costumes marched in a predominantly Hispanic San Francisco neighborhood known as the Mission District. The parade stopped at various "stations of the sun" that the organizers had created. They gave out oranges to symbolize the sun and played handmade rhythm instruments and cowbells while they walked and danced. A large group of neighborhood residents decided to join in the festivities.

The themes of sun, dance, music, costume, and masquerade were perfectly suited to the Carnaval's intention. The parade attracted a Panamanian dance instructor at the Mission Cultural Center longing for her lost childhood in her home country, longings that channeled Minor's embrace of the exotic into a different direction. Joined by a New York–born Panamanian Jamaican, the three decided to organize a "Carnivalito" in the Mission. Following the carnival's Roman Catholic roots, the event was held during the pre-Lenten period of February 1979 and was modeled on Afro-Caribbean and Afro-Latin traditions. The participants included a dance troupe, Chicano musicians and dancers, and drummers from Cuba. The event drew around 1,000 participants, many wearing masks and costumes. From the beginning, the organizers tried to make Carnaval racially inclusive and to attract participants from "a variety of traditions." Their intention was to include "more traditional Carnival cultures as well as others which had *some* kind of celebratory traditions, if not specifically Carnival traditions"

(Minor 1997). They received support and assistance from local artists, many of whom were from the Mission's Latino community. African American participation was minimal, and white participation was limited, even though a number of "delighted old Irish church ladies" (remnants of the large Irish population that claimed the Mission before the Latinos) attended the first Carnaval (Minor 1997). The event attracted several thousand people, mostly from the Mission, and culminated in a gathering and celebration in a neighborhood park.

After the success of the 1979 event, the Precita Park Neighborhood Center in the Mission began to contribute support and assistance, making possible a second, more elaborate, Carnaval in 1980. This one was a street affair, ending up in a large park in the Mission District. This time there was a more determined effort to draw in other neighborhoods and groups. As a result, the event attracted around 15,000 participants. Soon the West Indian community began carving out its own "space" in the festivities, after a Trinidadian with ties to the San Francisco Arts Council became involved. Thereafter, the Carnaval developed from a neighborhood festival into a parade to downtown City Hall. In 1985, its organization was taken over by the Mission Economic and Cultural Association, and the Brazilian community began to take center stage. According to one of its organizers and publicists, the parade now represents "Brazilians, Afro-Caribbeans, and Latin Americans, in that order" (interview with Chris Collins 1979). Thus, Carnaval has been transformed into a symbolic publicization of immigrant communities from African-based and African-influenced countries, even though the organizers continue to emphasize the representations of all "Third World" immigrant communities. This link to other "Third World" communities is essential to publicizing the location of the West Indian, Brazilian, and Latino communities in the social space occupied by non-Americanized immigrants.

Since its inception, the San Francisco Carnaval has grown quickly, attracting more than 600,000 spectators from the Bay Area and beyond. The fifty-five to seventy parade entries have more than 10,000 participants, representing primarily the West Indian and Latin American immigrant communities plus some Africans and Filipinos. Nonetheless, the entries' composition is multiracial, with significant numbers of white American participants. Some floats and costume bands are even predominantly, and sometimes completely, white, despite representing West Indian or Latin cultural forms in dress, music, and other displays of exotica. Whites are particularly evident among the belly dancers and Brazilian samba groups. The presence of so many whites among the African dancers emphasizes their understanding of Carnaval as an African-based event, whereas they are noticeably absent from displays of the indigenous cultures of the Americas.

In sum, the audience for the Carnaval is overwhelmingly white. The number of African Americans is very small, and the parade is merely a passing curiosity to the Chicano community in the Mission District that they share with their Latino neighbors. But members of the Mexican immigrant community are well represented in the parade and among the spectators.

The San Francisco Carnaval has evolved into a two-day "celebration of food and music." Hundreds of pavilions and booths are set up at the end of the parade route. The food booths sell dishes from West Africa, New Orleans, El Salvador, the West Indies, and the Philippines, as well as American barbecue. Latin, salsa, calypso, and reggae bands, many from the Caribbean and Latin America, perform on several open-air stages. On the day of the parade, disk jockeys with amplified musical systems accompany the bands through the streets. When the parade is over, the bands settle among the pavilions and food stalls, attracting their special clientele.

For the West Indian community, the San Francisco Carnaval is the perfect arena for publicizing itself and its association with other immigrant communities, particularly Latin American and African. English-speaking West Indians are joined by West Indians from the French, Dutch, and Spanish Caribbean. Ethnic accommodation and the polyglot character of West Indian identity is signaled by the inclusion of Native American and Chicano performances in the parade, even though such inclusion is not matched by the presence of these communities in the audience and at the fair. What is demonstrated is the Afro-Caribbeans' openness.

The San Francisco Carnaval is definitively not "American" and, particularly for West Indians, not "African American." African American music, dance, food, and performance are noticeably absent. The sole exception (apart from a New Orleans and an American barbecue booth) is a major radio station in the Bay Area with a large African American audience which broadcasts live from the event. Its shift from its regular fare of hip-hop and R&B to African and Caribbean-based "world music" makes clear that the broadcast is intended for a non–African American audience. Most of the African Americans who participate in Carnaval already have contacts and identify with the West Indian community. For instance, one of the West Indian costume bands is organized and led by an African American woman whose years of association with West Indians have effectively transformed her into a West Indian. This association began with a friendship with a West Indian neighbor which escalated into almost total involvement in the affairs of the community to the point that she has virtually lost her African American identity.

The absence of African Americans among the predominantly white group of nonparticipants who flock to view the parade and to attend the food and music festival is not surprising, since to a large extent, the San Francisco Carnaval is public arena for the symbolic display of differences between West Indians, Africans, and other African-based immigrant communities, on the one hand, and African Americans, on the other. This also explains the main difference between the New York and San Francisco festivals in the composition of the participants and audience and their structure and location. Carnaval is, for West Indians in San Francisco, as much a demonstration of white accommodation and white embrace as it is of separation from the American racial discourse, predicated on the understanding of West Indians as exotic and foreign, albeit desirable and legitimate. These collective self-representations are not a statement of claim to ethnopolitical turf. There is no need to demonstrate a numerical presence. Nor is Carnaval a means of establishing a claim to an ethnogeographic location. Instead, the event signifies a festive, exotic accommodation of white America.

Afribbean Festival in Silicon Valley

The differences between "West Indianness" and "blackness" are much more evident at the Afribbean Festival. This is actually two weekend music and cultural festivals, one held in the town of Mountain View in July and the second in the city of San Jose in August, both in the heart of Silicon Valley in Santa Clara County. The festival combines the African-centered orientations of the African American community with Afro-Caribbean and Afro-Latin cultural representations. It also incorporates the agenda of social responsibility typical of the African American middle class. Accordingly, the African American presence in its organization, cultural presentation, performance, and participation is significant. These are the features that distinguish the Afribbean Festival from the New York Carnival and the San Francisco Carnaval (much of the information about the Afribbean Festival was provided by its organizer, Jetin Grewal, in interviews in 2000).

African Americans comprise a mere 3.6 percent of Santa Clara's population, but many black professionals live and work in Silicon Valley, though outside East Palo Alto, which is known as a "black town." They are scattered throughout Santa Clara and come from everywhere in the African diaspora, with the majority being African American. But their diversity and their scattered locations, plus their relatively small numbers, have prevented the formation of networks of association and affinity based on national or regional origin.

Like the New York and San Francisco festivals, the Afribbean Festival emerged from the specific interests of a few people. But soon it became the largest and most important publicization of the diverse mixture of persons of African descent and the primary arena for their symbolic self-representation.

Jetin Grewal, an immigrant from India, and her European American husband started the Afribbean Festival in 1993 as a way of bringing together Santa Clara's scattered Afro-Caribbean community. In its first year, the event was held in a small parking lot behind a nightclub in Mountain View. It attracted between 5,000 and 6,000 persons. In 1994, the festival moved to the downtown area of Mountain View, now attracting an audience of more than 20,000. In 1998, it became a two-day weekend event, and San Jose was added as a second venue. By 2000, the Afribbean Festival was attracting a combined audience of more than 255,000.

While initially organized for the Afro-Caribbean community, the event quickly assumed its diasporic character, following the original intention of the two organizers. They selected the name "Afribbean" in order to celebrate the cultural arts and music of the Caribbean and Africa. The evolution of its African-centered character was prompted by the influence of the county's African American population. There was considerable opposition to the festival by Mountain View's city officials, and on several occasions, they attempted to deny permission for its continuation as an annual event. To ensure its survival, the organizers had to enlist the social and political influence of the organized African American community and the festival's supporters, including the African Family Foundation; the Santa Clara County Black Chamber of Commerce; KBLX—a black-oriented radio station specializing in R&B, jazz, and classical soul music; and the Green Party.

The Afribbean Festival is not a typical carnival; rather, it is a cultural fair highlighting the arts and culture of Africa, the Afro-Caribbean, and Afro-Latin America. It has no street parade but instead emphasizes the sale of arts, crafts, and ethnic foods. Many businesses and public agencies use the event to hire employees and to advertise and introduce their goods and services to the black community. The Afribbean Festival is, in essence, an Africa-centered event that incorporates the social agenda of the African American middle class.

The main stage at the festival features African bands as well as bands from the Caribbean and Latin and Central America. Community drum circles occupy a central place in the festivities, with participants encouraged to "bring your drums and join the fun." Once again, the emphasis is on Africa. Elements of the West Indian carnival announce the West Indian presence as integral to the event. A "Carnival Showcase and Parade" features presentations by the masquerade and dance bands from the San Francisco Carnaval.

The Afribbean Festival is an event at which the black professional and middle classes join the liberal community to celebrate and publicize the success of persons of African descent in Silicon Valley. Success is indicated by a display of black spending power, through which "businesses get an opportunity to participate in a celebration that enhances their economic growth and visibility to a niche market." Those in attendance are expected to spend considerable sums of money. The event attracts upward of 265 vendors, who sell ethnic arts, crafts, clothes, jewelry, housewares, and food.

The festival publicizes the social commitment of successful African Americans to the black community and their association with the racial mix of liberals. Its functional emphasis is on raising funds to support educational programs for African American youths. In 1997, Grewal formed a nonprofit organization called Global Culture and Arts, Inc. In addition to organizing the Afribbean Festival and other "culturally enhancing events," the organization actively supports "educational and cultural programs in schools, implement outreach programs for youths and adults, and facilitate diversity focused seminars and workshops." Revenue from the festival goes to a number of programs, such as a tutoring program in math and science taught by Stanford University graduate and undergraduate students, a jazz ensemble and workshop, an African American youth and family summit, a youth forum, a girls' middle-school dance program, and an African American caucus (Afribbean website).

The negative stereotypes of African Americans, reinforced in the popular images of East Palo Alto, are refuted by the Afribbean Festival as a crime-free, sober, "family-related event." Organizers "encourage families to attend and to bring their kids along." The festival is showcased as a "forum [where] friends and families get together in a harmonious and peaceful atmosphere." A "Learning Tree Stage" provides entertainment for children through puppet shows, African storytelling, clown performances, drumming, and face painting. Despite sponsorship from beer and rum companies, "alcohol abuse [does] not appear to be a problem," even though there is no special effort to control drinking (see Allen-Taylor 1998). This image of moderation and self-restraint differs sharply from that associated with the African American lower class. Everything emphasizes this class distinction, including the absence of cultural forms identified with the African American lower class. The organizers do not feature hip-hop music, although it is played at two small booths selling music. Despite considerable pressure, Grewal chose to exclude rap and blues performances from the festival. She explains this by pointing out the many festivals that do offer this type of entertainment.

Afribbean is also a publicization of the black presence in technology. A "Digital Village" shows the latest innovations in computer and communications technology. Attendees are given opportunities to exchange ideas on a "real-time basis with people from around the world." Videoconferencing and Internet uses are demonstrated, and the festival is shown on the Internet. On display as well are many high-tech booths representing companies such as Cisco Systems, Pacific Bell, and Innetix Wireless (Afribbean website).

Between 70 and 80 percent of those in attendance are black, the majority being African Americans. Their predominance is evident in the kinds of groups and organizations involved with the festival. In addition, two African Americans, one Nigerian, one West Indian, two South Asians, and one white American are on its organizing committee.

The Afribbean Festival is a representation of the aspirations of the black middle and professional classes and a publicization of their self-representation. It is presented as a more "upscale" event than its San Francisco counterpart, because it is centered on the black professional presence in Silicon Valley. Its class character is communicated through the incorporation of the social responsibility and community service typical of the African American elite, and it confirms its association with the multiracial liberal community.

For all these reasons, the Afribbean Festival is perfectly suited to the communication of the West Indian middle class's identific aspirations and self-understandings. The relationship between the West Indian professional middle class and its African American counterpart has led to the adoption of the African American elite's social agendas. West Indian professionals depend on networks established by African Americans for access, protection, and upward mobility in their careers and occupations. This professional association, however, does not detract from the self-representations of the West Indian middle class as a model minority.

In Silicon Valley, minorities use ethnonational networks and organizations to enhance their income and occupational status. African Americans are at the organizational core of the black professional networks and associations in Silicon Valley, and West Indian professionals benefit from them. They also depend professionally on the informal networks organized by African Americans in the industries and companies where they are employed. Their participation fosters association, collegiality, and friendship ties with their African American professional colleagues, relationships that are publicized through the West Indian representation in the Afribbean Festival. The festival's African-centered theme is consistent with the willingness of the black educated elite to develop an African-centered diasporic identity. As an exhibition of the social and political power of the African American middle and professional classes, the Afribbean Festival is a public confirmation of their importance to the success of the West Indian "model minority."

Conclusion

The West Indian immigrant identity is formed from social, political, economic, and situational contexts. Symbols, rituals, and performance combine in self-representations of highly contextualized identity constructs. At the most general level, festivals and parades provide arenas for publicizing collective self-representations. Through performance and displays, they assert and communicate their collective identity.

West Indians in the United States use exotic images in the performance and display of identity, consistent with popular American understandings of "West Indianness." While similar in form, the various carnivals signify fundamentally different cognitive constructs of West Indian identity. These constructs are responding to the contextualized demands of the different locations where West Indians live. In New York, the carnival announces the West Indians' insertion into the American ethnic mix, reflecting the pattern of incorporation followed by other ethnic Americans. In San Francisco, the Carnaval provides a venue for communicating a West Indian immigrant and foreign presence outside the racial discourse of American society. In negotiating their identity, West Indians have had to forgo incorporation into the America milieu. and the San Francisco Carnaval publicizes this separation from the American nationalist identity. In Santa Clara, however, the Afribbean Festival publicizes the relationship between the West Indian and the African American professional classes and refutes the African American stereotypes.

The preceding three case studies of carnivals highlight the manner in which social, economic, cultural and political factors combine in the construction of identific representation and practice. In all three cases, these carnivals' performances have been used in the publicization of identity.

3

Promoters of Popular Culture

The culture of identity is produced in a sociogeographic arena, in which it is organized around the activities of those persons who are publicizing it. They are responsible for interpreting the meaning of the collective presence of an identific community. They do this by developing and presenting the symbols, rituals, and performances that become signifiers of the popular understanding.

Collective self-representations of popular culture are derived from the cognitive constructs of the identific community that exist in the popular consciousness, and they respond to the general understandings of the community being identified. Thus they represent the collective conscience and reflect the changing outcomes of identity negotiation.

The need to publicize this collective identity creates opportunities for those who want to organize and fashion its public displays. They become the promoters of popular culture. Some bring to the particular sociogeographic arena experience in the particular forms of popular cultural production that symbolize and represent the collective identity. Others may seek opportunities to fill the need for publicization. For example, the promotion of popular culture might serve as a means of social insertion into the community or might provide access to economic opportunity.

The promoters of popular culture are at the center of identity construction. Without them, the identific community would remain invisible and incoherent. Its members might be viewed as "strange," "idiosyncratic," or even "bizarre." The role of these promoters, then, is to transmit popular knowledge about the group and to publicize its legitimate presence in a particular sociogeographic arena. They normalize the existence of members of the identific community and create the basis for establishing cognitive links between, on the one hand, the group's collective behavior and, on the other hand, popular understandings about the group.

In many instances, it is the agency of these promoters that moves them from the margins of the identific community into its mainstream. Some may lack the social and economic attributes around which the group's identity is organized and understood. Or they may lack legitimate access to the arena in which the group is located. Their role as cultural promoters thus may serve to underwrite their legitimacy within the larger sociogeographic arena and within the identific community itself.

Legality and socioeconomic success are hallmarks of the West Indian identity in the San Francisco Bay Area, and the absence of either can lead to marginalization and social isolation. *Legality* refers to both immigrant status and activities that violate the law. Thus, undocumented persons constantly live in fear of exposure. Isolation and marginalization are inevitable without an institutionalized network of protection from discovery. Such a network is usually organized by the immigrant community itself. But no such network exists in the Bay Area for West Indians; in fact, those engaged in illegal activities are avoided and shunned. Social exclusion is not confined, however, to those breaking the law. West Indian immigrants in California who live outside the ambit of social and economic success may find themselves excluded from the private and semiprivate arenas where identity is produced. Their role as promoters of popular culture may give them, though, another means of access to the community when they become central to its production and publicization of identity.

James Taylor

James Taylor came to the United States in the 1970s with his fiancée and their young child, on a tourist visa but with the intention of remaining in the country. Because he had had postsecondary semiprofessional training in his country of origin, he was able to enter as a skilled worker. A member of his country's relatively impoverished lower class, he had been forced as an adolescent to work at menial odd jobs to support himself and help support his family. But his parents' emphasis on education paid off, and he was able to become a certified technician. Although he found a well-paying job, he began to worry about job security when his baby was born and also to look for more out of life: "I had no need to come to the United States. But I looked into the future."

He first tried to settle in New York but became frustrated with his marginal existence: "Coming as an immigrant, I don't have a green card. It was very frustrating to me. Crime was one of the greatest concerns I had to deal with in the streets of New York, almost immediately." The situation became even more desperate with the birth of a second child. So on a whim, he decided to move to California.

This began James's search for social and cultural roots. He attempted, unsuccessfully, to enter the network of undocumented Latinos. But he encountered what he described as extreme "racism" on the part of a Hispanic or white family (he was not sure which they were) with whom he lived with his fiancée and their children, under circumstances that he did not reveal. After three weeks in California, he left for a large city in the southern United States and began what he described as a life of a "nomad." However, he was severely constrained by his undocumented status and quickly "realized that I had to get myself legal." Accordingly, he met and married an American woman and was able to secure his permanent residence status. In his own words, "It was a blast from the time I got my green card." After he "got a good job" on the basis of his semiprofessional training, he divorced his American wife and married his former fiancée. Two years later, he lost his job because of budgetary cuts, which precipitated a series of moves to other southern and northwestern cities. He took a series of unskilled and semiskilled jobs and sometimes was forced to live on welfare. James finally managed to obtain a number of well-paying jobs, despite constantly moving from city to city, unable to settle down. The pressures and frustrations of his nomadic existence took a toll on his family. After five years of marriage and five children, his wife decided to leave him.

James's self-understandings were firmly located in the social culture of his country of origin, and this seemed to be the cause of his restlessness and his constant movement. His wife appeared to be the only unchanging link to his origins. Indeed, after his resident status was legalized, James immediately sought a job with a company with contracts in his homeland. The job brought with it an opportunity for periodic visits home as a liaison for the company. It also provided the financial security that he sought. His bosses "flew me back and I was to introduce them. So from living in poverty, now I'm staying in one of the biggest hotels downtown in the capital, introducing these American businesspeople to our local businesspeople. It was a blast." Clearly, James was trying to recover his origins while securing a financially sound future for himself and family. Before he was eventually laid off, he was transferred to a city with a large West Indian population.

This is how James explained his first move to California:

> I became somewhat of a nomad looking for better opportunities, a better place to raise my family. So economics [was] one of the factors. Socially, where I was able to interact with other Caribbean people. I looked for a place that lent that kind of thing, a climate compared to where I was born. So I moved to California, my very first move.

James was embarked on a search for his roots, which explains his "nomadic" life.

With his moves to locations with no West Indians and no opportunities to return home, James's wife became the only remaining link to his sociocultural roots and country of origin. Her departure, therefore, proved to be quite a traumatic experience, and James's reaction was to give up his job and return to his homeland in search of another wife: "So I took a flight to my country, to see if I can find out what—I actually went looking for a wife. Can you imagine that?" Clearly, he had changed.

> I couldn't deal with the level of intelligence of the people I was meeting [at home]. When I left there, it was OK. After about six years or five years, you go back home and you're looking to talk to somebody, and they're talking about cooking. Global events—or current events—it's just not [one of their concerns]. I couldn't deal with it. I don't know if I went to the wrong place. I decided I would get out of there.

What he decided to do instead was to move to California.

California offered a West Indian community that seemed successful, educated, and well paid. It combined those elements of the cultural roots he was seeking with the ideals of achievement that he wanted. Although James arrived with considerable savings, he had little of the cultural capital (in the form of acquired knowledge, education, skills, and capabilities) that defined the West Indian community there. For his economic survival, he depended on own-account buying and selling, which placed him just above the level of a vendor. This he chose to hide from his West Indian associates, who began to speculate about the source of his income. The uncertainty of his socioeconomic status and his source of income became reasons for his marginalization from the network of West Indians.

James was prevented by financial obligations to his family from seeking a higher education that would unequivocally secure him a place in the West Indian community. Instead, he was forced to remain constantly on the move in search of jobs that required little skill but paid high wages. This is how he explained one of his moves:

> I scouted the area and I realized I could make money here. I got a job with a contractor and started making something like $40 an hour, but I'm working out in the cold. So I'm working two weeks, so I'm making $40 something an hour, and then I'm home for two weeks. When I'm home, I started working another job in the fishing industry. So now I'm working for $22 an hour. So I kept working, working, working, and working. I moved my family up and everything. The kids went and started enrolling in school. I think my son was in kindergarten up there. We had five kids. So we come up there and I was working all the time.

So when he moved to California, James had financial security, but his search for the familiarity of his "roots" continued to be frustrated by his marginalization on the fringes of the West Indian community:

> I have some West Indians—very few West Indians. I know a lot of people who are West Indians and everybody probably knows me. But we do not sit and break bread together and sit and have drinks. But if we are out, we are going to sit and have a great conversation. That's the kind of relations I have with Caribbean people here.

James saw himself as having very little in common with African Americans. His stereotypical images of them precluded any relationship with members of that community. He declared himself "threatened by many black people—by the way they dress, when they come on my car." And he saw the need for a strategy to deal with them that demanded their respect for him. At the time of the interview, James was living in an African American neighborhood and felt the need to "set boundaries" to ensure his own survival:

> They come to you and say, could I have money for my drugs or anything like that, and you look them in the eye and you say, I wish I could but I don't have it, and you're straight up with them—they give you respect.

To deal with his isolation, James decided to marry a North African, but the relationship did not last. He also lost most of his money and so decided to resume his nomadic life. He returned to the San Francisco

Bay Area a few years before the interview took place, and it was then that he decided to become involved in the music industry.

> I got a chance to clear my head. Then I came back and I decided I'm going to go back into what I like, which is music. I'm going to be good at what I like. So I came back [for] about a year and I just spent about $50,000 to $60,000—I know it's more—on equipment, and I went back into what I like—which is music and sound.

Music was clearly the path back to his cultural roots. It was also his means of entering the West Indian community. But his marginalization posed a dilemma. He recognized that people "hold on to their traditions, their values—be [they] spiritual, cultural, economical, or whatever—they're keeping their money in their own community, they're having their own newspaper, their own radio stations, and whatever. I think that's good. But for me as a West Indian, I do not have the base in my community." He resolved the dilemma by using his music to become a cultural ambassador:

> I market myself as a Caribbean person here, where diversity is something I embrace. So I sell my music. I provide music for a lot of corporations, giving them a historical view—not only listening to music but giving them a lot of knowledge about the culture by way of dance, by way of history. When you come to something that I do in the way of music, I always give some sort of an insight as to what this is all about. I find the greater portion of the population here in the United [States] has a greater appreciation for that. That's most of the white people. So most of my work is catered to that audience more so than my own Caribbean audience.

While asserting his West Indian identity, James also understood the class basis of his marginalization from the West Indian community. Indeed, the image of the successful Asian seemed to inform his own assessments of their attitude toward him, and these assumed attitudes, in turn, dictated his own understanding of his relations with the Asian community:

> I look at the Asians, I see these are people who don't like black people at all—whether you're Mexican black, Trinidad black, American black—they do not really respect you. When I say Asian, I say it across the board. I say Filipinos, I say Chinese, I say Japanese. As a black coming from the Caribbean, you don't get the kind of equal respect. There is a profile that they put you in that they think you fit. You have to excel a lot socially. Even when they can visualize [you] by your attire, they will

allow [you] a little respect but they will not give you full respect—those are my views.

On the other hand, he felt considerable affinity with the Latino population, to what he perceived in its position in California's social economy that was identical to his own.

> I love Latin people. I tend to have good relations with Latin people. I play a lot of salsa. I sung in a lot of salsa bands. I've learned that Latin people are people who are working—they want to work. Latin people have that sense of having that nuclear family. A lot of rhythm. I think they have the best people to work with. They will come and say, we want to do this but we don't really have much. But when we grow, you'll grow with us—and I find that they hold their word more in business than black people. If you have a Latin friend and you are their friend, my experience—be it male or female—they will be with you all the way.

James understands himself as a West Indian in terms quite similar to his images of Latinos. That is, he is someone who has worked hard and so can make it in the United States:

> America is a place, with the experience I have as I look back today, America is a place if you work as a West Indian coming here and you follow the laws of the land—and you market yourself, whatever product you're marketing—and you market yourself, you will be successful. America will give you what you put into it. In the midst of all its problems—be it unfair treatment to minorities—if you present yourself and you package everything about you right, America will not bother with you.

James sees the West Indian community as an impediment to his own success. In other immigrant communities, "people are still holding on to their traditions, their values—be it spiritual, cultural, economical or whatever—they're keeping their money in their own community, they're having their own newspaper, their own radio stations, and whatever." This is certainly not the case in the West Indian community:

> I think we have a crush in our social way of dealing with each other, whether it's lack of trust, whether it's to gain the friendship of others. We will speak ill of each other and put each other down more so than saying uplifting things of one another. I think when we have members of our community excelling, instead of we as a people rallying around those people—those fractions or whatever—we tend to, as a people, find it necessary to degrade them. It could cause morale to go low and if you don't have a support base in anything you do, you have problems—be it

a financial one, be it buddies—as members of a community you have a problem.

Despite his self-description as a "marketer" of West Indian culture, James tried hard to end his own marginalization. As he earned more money from his music production and his activities as a small scale-entrepreneur, he was able to buy a house in a middle-class community. He began hosting semipublic parties exclusively for the West Indian community and established a highly visible presence in West Indian public events, such as the San Francisco Carnaval, the Afribbean Festival in Santa Clara, and all West Indian musical and cultural activities.

James's marginalization was based on his socioeconomic profile. Because of the financial pressures of having a family, he was unable to continue in school. He was, however, able to find high-paying jobs and used the money to support a number of small business ventures, many of which failed. Only when he had some economic security and could become a cultural promoter was James able to join the West Indian network. His membership, however, was as a functionary; he still was excluded from the more intimate private gatherings. He still did not "break bread" with members of the West Indian community.

Sidney Shelton

If they are successful, cultural promoters have a critical presence in their own community, especially when they provide desired linkages with other communities. The reason is that cultural promoters can publicize the patterns of relations that an identific community wants to emphasize when negotiating a desired location in the sociocultural order. Indeed, many see themselves as possessing the means to act as cultural bridges.

Sidney Shelton arrived in the United States in the mid-1970s as a permanent resident when a rich white family sponsored his mother for employment as a housekeeper. He moved to New York but was unable to settle down and began longing for what he described as his idyllic life at home: "I was playing music, basketball, soccer, cricket, karate. Oooh weee, busy, busy. It was good. It was really good." His memories of the town from which he came were equally idealized. He described it as having the "flavor of not only you're in the Caribbean, the temperature, but this old modern, what you call it, I lost the words, but basically the town had this kind of antique, old English style, the big clock, the big, and then we were still able to get necessities, food and running water was not a problem." As soon as he arrived in the United States, Sidney immediately began making plans to return home, but his country's political problems stood in the way.

It was Sidney's longing for home that made him decide to move to California. "I was searching for a better life . . . [and] felt New York was not it." He was persuaded to stay after visiting a friend in the Bay Area: "A friend of mine, classmates in school, came here first. He stayed in Concord, and through a phone call to Brooklyn where I was living one evening, he talked about it. We got back to it at the end of the evening and I started deciding maybe, because there are a lot of things in California, I'm coming."

Sidney came without qualifications and skills. He settled in one of the Bay Area suburbs which reminded him of home, and he eventually got a job as a semiskilled technician, receiving on-the-job training, supplemented by courses that he took at a community college. To earn additional income, he quickly began using his knowledge of and familiarity with Caribbean music to get a job as a Caribbean disk jockey, and he was astute enough to target his music to the growing white audience. He also began to participate in a number of Caribbean activities and organizations and to associate with some of the Caribbean students at the Bay Area's colleges and universities. These students gave him his link to the West Indian network. His own economic position was not much different from theirs; indeed, it was somewhat better. So his presence in this segment of the West Indian community was not unusual, and he became a central figure on a number of West Indian cricket teams and, through them, was able to become even more firmly established in community affairs. His music increased his popularity and won him invitations to private and semipublic functions. Soon he began to promote events that attracted mixed audiences interested in West Indian music. At the same time, his wife enrolled in a community college and, after graduating, transferred to one of the Bay Area's universities. Eventually, she earned a professional degree and a well-paying job in a highly respected field. They bought a house in one of the suburbs and became well known as hosts for social gatherings. With their savings, they began to invest in a number of West Indian clubs and restaurants catering to diverse audiences. Their ventures featured a "family atmosphere" and diversity, with an emphasis on African-based entertainment that had widespread appeal. The diversity of these venues, signified by their white and immigrant clientele (the latter mainly from Asia and Africa) publicized West Indians' distinctiveness from African Americans.

Sidney saw himself as particularly suited to be a cultural ambassador. He claimed to have a "mixed" black, Asian, and white racial background but felt most closely connected to white America, with which he had "never had a problem." In fact, the white presence in California was one of the things that attracted him to the state: "the feel of people from Berkeley, and Oakland, and Richmond and El Sobrante and then San Francisco, and Concord." He explained whites' acceptance of West Indians:

> White folks might have traveled, so there was always the capital to do things like that, and if they don't go to the Caribbean, they may go to Europe. And in Europe, there's a lot of Caribbean folks, people too. So, they might run across us in the ship, in our countries, or in other countries and find that, hmm, black folks is not too bad.

Sidney found an affinity with every other ethnic group except African Americans, and this affinity was reflected in his ventures:

> I had the fortune of working closely with almost every ethnic group. Party with them, work professionally with them, and I never had any problems. I mean, I had a group over in San Francisco who came to my business every Friday, and they would bring twenty or thirty people, Asians, come right in to the party and drink, because it kind of, atmosphere from the surroundings, you know, we associate ourselves with, the Asians. We are very inclusive. And so people don't feel like there is tension so, if you have nothing to fear about, you kind of, let your feelings flow and that's what I find with every group, Latinos, Asians.

Sidney defined himself, openly, in ways that distinguished him from African Americans. When asked about his relationship with African Americans, he recounted in the interview an experience at work:

> I was told again this week, at my job, they tease a lot about race around there, because I'm the kind of guy I can take it, but I give it too. I let them know I'm proud of who I am. But, they always, this joke started one time, and I said, "I'm not black. I'm chocolate. No, I'm cocoa." And so they always think, what's wrong with you? Scared of a black man. What

are you talking about? You are cocoa, remember? You are cocoa. And so, I don't know.

He went on to emphasize his obvious difference from African Americans:

I think my accent has something to do with it. I know somebody white will comment. They will tell right away, you're not American. I think there's an automatic respect. You probably would listen more, want to hear, What's he going to say next?

But Sidney did express concern about the presence of African Americans at his cultural ventures, because they had a "chip on their shoulder" that West Indians did not have.

As a cultural promoter, Sidney organized the activities through which the West Indian community would meet and engage in identific rituals. He used his cultural and economic resources to publicize the social position of West Indians in the successful immigrant communities. The cultural activities that he organized symbolized the community's accommodation of whites. Thus, Sidney was able to join the Bay Area's West Indian community without having the social markers of West Indian success. The reason was his central role in the identific construction of West Indian identity. To this was added the professional attributes of his wife's success, consistent with West Indian self-representations. Sidney thus was able to parlay his role as cultural promoter into economic success.

Janet Jason

When immigrants arrive with a strong sense of identity, social isolation from their community can heighten their cultural sensibilities and lead to their becoming cultural promoters in order to gain access. That is, they may be accepted because of their efforts to reproduce their community.

There are many reasons for social isolation. In James's and Sidney's cases, their socioeconomic status conflicted with the self-understandings of West Indians in the San Francisco Bay Area. But even those whose socioeconomic and cultural attributes fit the community's self-image may not escape social isolation, for the circumstances of their immigration can lead to marginalization and social isolation.

Janet Jason immigrated to California at the urging of her brother and his wife, both of whom were successful professionals. Her brother was the head of a large department in a state agency, and his wife, who had both a Ph.D. and a professional graduate degree, was a senior manager in a major organization. They also owned real estate throughout the Bay Area and had an affluent lifestyle.

Janet's brother and his wife were deeply involved in the African American network of professionals in their fields. Indeed, the politics and social expectations of her brother's position demanded sensitivity to, involvement with, and engagement with the black community. His was, to a certain extent, a "black" position, and his wife had found it necessary to use the black network of professionals to rise in her profession. Like her African American counterparts, she was quite outspoken on issues of race and had developed an Africa-centered ideological orientation. She began to visit Africa and wear African clothing. At the same time, she criticized the West Indian community for what she saw as its "backwardness" on racial issues. She was also critical of the West Indies for not developing its professions, particularly her own.

This was the environment to which Janet was introduced when she decided to immigrate. Her initial reason for coming was to attend one of the Bay Area's community colleges. Janet had a strong sense of her West Indianness:

> My roots are in the Caribbean. I still can't feel a part of America. I don't know if it's because I can't relate to the ancestry of America. Because I don't know what it is. It's so diverse. I feel a sense of belonging to the West Indies. Even though I am a citizen of the U.S., I can't call myself an American.

She also felt a deep sense of loss for having come to the United States:

> I've had to give up my standard of life. Because my standard of life, as I mentioned earlier, has fallen. I had to give up . . . I had to leave my immediate family. So I lost out on the past fifteen years with my immediate family. Even though we stayed in touch, it's not the same as being there.

The first time that Janet came to America, she stayed for only two years and returned to the West Indies without completing her education. She claimed that her "mind was not on school." After she returned to the West Indies, she got married, apparently using the marriage as an excuse to go home: "I was madly in love. And the person I was in love with was back home." But the marriage did not last, and she settled down into a relatively comfortable life after getting a job and moving up to a management position in a small company.

Janet decided to settle permanently in the United States after coming on a tourist visa in the early 1980s and being encouraged by her brother and his wife to stay. She explained her decision as a desire to be with her grandmother: "I chose the United States because that's where my grandmother was living. And I always wanted to be close to my grandmother, because she is the person who I feel is responsible for me being alive."

Janet's sister-in-law introduced her to an African American, and they decided to get married because "in order to stay, I had to get married, but we ended up making a go of it." She saw her marriage in almost functional terms: "I stayed married for ten years, which was a great accomplishment because I was able to finish my studies and do all I wanted to do and get that out of the way." Apart from getting an education, she seemed to view her presence in the United States as an extended vacation: "I like to do lots of camping and driving around. My goal really is to drive around America by road. That's my goal."

The marriage increased her isolation from the West Indian community. Her brother's and his wife's almost exclusive involvement in the professional and social circle of African Americans also worked against her introduction to the Bay Area's network of West Indians, as they stayed away from the West Indian community and its affairs. Janet's connections to the West Indies were thus confined to social gatherings of family members who either had moved to the Bay Area or came to visit during the holidays. To compensate, she began to make numerous trips back home, sometimes more than once every year.

Janet's job was in the department headed by her brother, and she also enrolled in one of the Bay Area's universities, earning a degree in business administration. But differences in tastes, style, and cultural practices began to strain her marriage, and Janet began making efforts to introduce her African American husband to the West Indian lifestyle. She encouraged him to visit the different islands in the region. But on these visits, he would engage in activities that he liked and with which he felt comfortable rather than those associated with a Caribbean lifestyle.

In the Bay Area, Janet's social circle proved to be quite restrictive, as it prevented her from becoming fully involved with the West Indian community. She therefore became a cultural promoter as a means of breaking out of this social isolation. After getting her degree, she decided to go into business and encouraged her husband to invest in the venture, a retail market that specialized in the sale of West Indian items, including foods. Her business quickly developed into a gathering place for the West Indian community, even though her intention was to introduce West Indian consumer culture to the Bay Area. She made a great effort to attract a diverse clientele.

Janet's business became a springboard for her greater participation in the West Indian community's social and cultural activities:

> I go to house parties, house gatherings, because we don't have very many Caribbean clubs. But whenever one would come up, I would support it. I try to stay in touch with all the cultural events that would be going on. We live for the Caribbean. I make a conscious effort, and I am pretty successful, to take part in carnivals in the Mission and things like that. And that way you get to hear of new people who have come, and you try to meet them and greet them.

Janet began sponsoring and organizing one of the West Indian masquerade bands for the San Francisco Carnaval, and she provided space at her business for the band's use. She also became an organizer and official in a Caribbean association.

Her husband viewed his wife's business only as a money-making venture, so when its cultural orientation began to affect its profitability, he decided to pull out, forcing Janet to sell it. The problem was caused by Janet's fundamentally different understanding of the role of the business, which she began using as a means of recreating West Indian cultural forms in the Bay Area. At the same time, she began to go back to the West Indies more frequently. The interview was conducted when she had just returned from two and a half months in her country of origin. She was going home at least once a year for an extended stay. On these trips, she usually "visit[ed] friends in the other islands. I would always visit the other islands." But when her business collapsed, she could not remain culturally and socially active. She described her current relationship with the community as "distant. I hear through other friends what's going on, but I'm not an active participant right now." Her response to her inevitable isolation was to spend even more time in the West Indies.

It is clear that Janet became a cultural promoter in order to reconstruct her idyllic image of her life in the Caribbean. Her business provided the base from which she could propel herself into the community and out of her social isolation. It also secured her husband's involvement. Her business legitimized her involvement in the self-representations of the West Indian community when she was not on one of her frequent visits home.

Janet's role as a cultural promoter differs from James's and Sidney's, who were seeking a way of joining the West Indian community. Janet, however, was seeking an escape from America. She did not think it was possible "for a black person to live in America and not experience racism." In her country, "it still is consoling to know that your prime minister is black; your cabinet is black. The persons who run the stores, they're black. When you turn on your television, it's black people. That's still a bit more consoling than it is here."

Janet's reaction to the United States had much to do with her family's involvement with the African American community. In the interview, she spent a lot of time describing American racism and her personal experiences with it. Her opinions reflected the general understandings of African Americans about their own position in American society and their experiences of racism. But she saw her West Indian identity as a foil: "I feel that I've been spared some of it [by] not being African American. When I speak, my accent tends to shield me from some of the racism that an African American might experience."

Tom Lander

Cultural activism can serve as a means of recapturing a West Indian identity, and it can be the basis for rituals of purification after reentering one's original identific community. Certain social and institutional contexts may impose specific identific constructs on its social participants and make the accommodation of alternative self-representations difficult or impossible.

The U.S. military places its members into specifically American categories. For example, immigrants must define themselves in American terms that are reflected in American understandings of difference and belonging. For West Indians, this means an imposed self-representation as African American. Once West Indians leave the military, however, they can reclaim their West Indian identity by means of intense cultural activism.

Tom Lander immigrated to the United States when he was twenty years old, bringing with him vivid images from the popular media.

I thought that America was the land where no wrong could be done, you know? You know the shows that we saw in the Caribbean, I have to admit, showed all the good side of America. You know, you saw your *Lassie*, you know, *Gunsmoke*, and all these shows that really showed more or less the upper hand of America, America being moralistic. You know, everybody's got a chance and all that good stuff. Which I suppose every country would show if they were going to export something, I don't know. I assume so.

Unlike the experience of many immigrants, Tom's first impressions of the United States were quite positive. He was fascinated by

the amount of things people had. The amount of just things. I mean, people just had a lot more. There was two cars. To me, I noticed two, sometimes three cars in the driveway, and that was like unknown. You walk into people's house, it's fully carpeted. So people just had a lot more stuff, you know. People just had houses. The kids had houses. People— like in America, at eighteen years, a person's looking to move out on their own.

Tom described his initiation into the United States as "culture shock" despite the excitement it generated. He described what he saw at the airport when he first arrived in New York:

Every one [was] white. Not by my country's standards, because in my country we have white people, but they're sort of mixed all the time. What we call white at home was nowhere white compared to what I was seeing. You know, so that was a shock to me. That was like—I mean, I stood up there, and I stared literally. I walked with my mouth open, and I just looked at these people. I was looking at *Lassie*, you know. I was like, "Wow, these people really exist!" So it was a shock to me. That was the first shock. And then my sister met me there, and I think I kind of— we drove home, and of course, the driving home, I'm seeing all these sights that I saw on television back home all the time, and I'm actually seeing them now, and my mouth is like—it's like "Wow!" So it was definitely a shock.

Eventually, the shock of the new environment began to produce a sense of social dislocation:

I really did not—was not prepared for the, the experience that I went through. I think in America, there's a variety of people and different dialects and tongues and in just one place. And then not knowing the person passing on the side of you and then realizing that you—you know you're seeing this person, and you're not probably ever going to know this person, and if you're going to introduce yourself to this person, it's not going to be like, you know, where you were back home where you'd know everybody, or you did know about them. You might not know them all personally, but within your area, you more or less knew everybody, and if anybody coming into the area was new, you could easily find out. In America, that's one of the things—the size of the place.

Tom also experienced a considerable degree of economic dislocation. He came from a solidly middle-class family in the West Indies. His father held a senior position in the country's civil service, and when he graduated from high school, he received the equivalent of an associate degree in a technical field before going to the United States. Nonetheless, he described his family as not being "financially able" in the United States. They had entered as legal permanent residents, and he came under his parents' sponsorship. But his family was struggling under the burden of low-paying service jobs in New York and the financial obligation of supporting one of his siblings, who was at college.

The need to regain some structure and stability, the opportunity to earn an income, and the possibilities for more technical training led Tom to join the military: "I should have tried to, you know, have [my family] send me through school and everything. [But the military] was the best opportunity at the time for me." He made the decision because he wanted an opportunity to continue to improve his technical skills and to use them.

Together, the excitement engendered by Tom's new experience in the United States and his sense of social dislocation from being in the country explain his choice of the military. It certainly gave him the security and stability that he wanted. Indeed, when his tour of duty was over, he enlisted in the National Guard, probably to retain the bounded predictability that he seemed to need. But the demands of the military caused him to reformulate his cultural self. Accordingly, he began dating African American women and eventually married one of them.

After leaving the military, Tom gave up the "big city life" of New York in favor of California. He described New York as a "concrete jungle." After a military posting in Southern California, he became convinced that it was the right place to settle: "Having been around the whole country, just about every state I'd been to, California was the place I always wanted to come. I actually was a resident of California, I had a California driver's license and everything from the first time I was here, and I always kept it, even though I went to other states." Tom decided to join his brother, who was a student in Northern California, and quickly used his technical training to obtain a well-paying job.

Immediately after being discharged, Tom became immersed in the affairs of the Caribbean community and began to shed all elements of the African American identity he had acquired in the military. He divorced his African American wife because the marriage had "never worked." He believed that he had gotten married "for the wrong reasons." He and his wife were "not compatible" because of "cultural differences," which he explained in the following way:

> I think American black women are very possessive of their men. Then again, the West Indian black man—he's more or less the head of his house, and he can—if he wants to go out and do something, go wherever, he goes. Go play soccer with the guys. She was staunch against that. So we had battles along those lines as far as what I could do when I wanted to do it, you know, and that was just some things that we went through that I think was just cultural differences. Things we ate, the music we listened to, everything was different, you know. The choice of friendship, everything. The shows we watched on TV, everything.

Tom believed that he had lost part of who he was by being in the United States.

> I think, I think I've lost some of my, my—I think I lost some of me, who I am, you know, to be quite frank. Who I am got lost and shuffled in the deck, you know. And the person I left, the person who left in 1979 is not the same person now because my experiences have been so different, and I've gone through so many things that I just—I don't think helped me as a person to grow, to become a better person. I kind of envy people who have stayed in my country of origin that way.

This realization fed what appeared to be a quest for identific purification. Almost immediately on arriving in the Bay Area, Tom began dating a West Indian woman, and they soon set up a household together. It was as if he wanted to get rid of the polluting effects of his marriage. He began actively promoting West Indian culture, first by becoming involved in the San Francisco Carnaval. He joined a West Indian masquerade band and assumed increasingly important roles in its administration, finally becoming president of the band's sponsoring organization. Tom also invested in a Caribbean restaurant. What this decision reveals is his strong cognitive association between food and Caribbean culture. Food had been his only remaining link with his West Indian identity during his military service:

> That's one thing I was always been able to do is cook, and so [in the military] I always, you know, would go and cook my own food when I was ready to eat some Caribbean food so I didn't have to wait and ask anyone. I would get in there and turn a good pot in a minute.

Tom organized his restaurant into a sort of center for Caribbean cultural performance and symbolic displays, and it also became the headquarters for his masquerade band and the location for West Indian functions. On the weekends, it was converted into a West Indian dance club. Tom also participated in the affairs of two Caribbean organizations, and for one, his restaurant sponsored twice weekly "musical songs" events. In the interview, he emphasized the cultural aspects of the two organizations.

Like Janet, Tom used his cultural promotions to recreate in the Bay Area his own version of the Caribbean, focusing on gatherings of people. His reminiscences of home were those of " the people, the friends that I have left behind that are still there. You know, we get together, we hang out, talk about old times, and go out and party and do this, just hang around." Later in the interview he returned to this subject:

> I kind of envy people who have stayed [in my country of origin] that way. But when I go back, you know, when I go back, you know, there's a certain type of warmth that you get immediately when you go back by just interrelating with people. They walk up to you and just talk to you. They don't do that in America. You don't go to the grocery and somebody just casually talk to you. "Oh, where did you get"—just talking to you, you know. It's not something that's done here.

> Here at [my] restaurant, we have a big kind of contingent [of people]. So that's another thing that goes on here. And this is like the home of the big Carnaval group. There's a pretty wide variety of people coming through these doors, and I'm pretty close to most of them.

Tom's desire to return to his country of origin was even stronger than Janet's. He explained his continued residence in the United States as typical of West Indians' desire for more training and education:

I have a couple things I have to finish up. I probably have to finish up school here, finish up, you know, all my schooling that I want to finish. You just never feel like you're finished until you—I mean, West Indian people, we've got to get to this point in our life where we have to have our education, you know. That's the stamp of success in the Caribbean, right? Educational level, and so that's something I have to do for me. If for nobody else, for me.

But as Janet did, Tom qualified his desire to return home:

I would like to start planting roots back home so that I have the option to go home when I want to go home, and then come back if I need to. I don't think I'm going to give this up completely because I'm going to reap as much as I can from this. Hey, that's the whole reason of coming to America, right? Get as much as you can. I mean, that's the good old greed. And there's nothing wrong with it, I suppose, and everybody's got to make it. And hopefully with this restaurant, I've got my break, and try to make this successful.

It is interesting that Tom uses the restaurant to explain his desire to retain some form of residency in the United States. Clearly, the activities organized around the restaurant represented an acceptable, if temporary, substitute for his life back home. These, and education, seemed in his mind to be the only terms under which living in the United States became acceptable.

Jason Roberts

Cultural promoters see themselves rooted in the lifestyles and folkways of their identified community, but they still, as immigrants, feel an association with their geosocial location. The immigrant presence in California has brought in its wake images and a popular consciousness of a multicultural ethos. This has led to an accommodation of difference and an understanding of the need for cultural bridging. Cultural promoters, therefore, may see themselves as performing these bridging functions, as translating their own cultural understanding to a welcoming audience from different identific communities. These persons may become quite sympathetic to their host communities. That is, their attitudes are both positive and neutral toward discourses of difference. At the same time, they do not see anything wrong with holding on to their own cultural practices while maintaining diverse associations.

Jason Roberts works in Silicon Valley as a technical professional and project manager in a high-tech division of a communications company. He has developed a dichotomized understanding of West Indians in the United States. One branch of the dichotomy is based on cultural and associational practices that are almost identical to Americans' exoticized popular understandings of West Indians. The second branch is that of the West Indian driven by the demands of success. Jason described these two elements of identity as two "types" of West Indian:

> There is the fun-loving West Indian. He loves to party. He loves to have a good time. He loves the culture. He would do anything to keep a lot of that culture, meaning, they're always in New York taking part in the festivities. They're in the Miami carnival. They're always going home. They may be involved in some kind of a steel band group as a professional or something of this sort. Then you also have the other side, which is more of the professional West Indian that is goal oriented and basically is pushing and driving to accomplish—has the "American Dream." You want the house. You want the car. You want the kids and all this good stuff.

What is clear is that the two "types" of West Indian refer to Jason himself. His cultural side is rooted in his deep sense of his West Indian identity. His "driven" side has much to do with his understanding of what America has offered him and his belief that it has fulfilled most of his desires, and at very little sacrifice. He describes life in America in positive terms, even though "it came with a price" in terms of family life:

> But you get the opportunity to have a nice car, a nice house, and all of these different material things. However, is the price that you pay for it—your family life—is it worth it? I don't know. But the standard of life, the utensils, the service, simple things like telephones, water, electricity, and all those various things, we are so more advanced—it is definitely better here.

Jason's attitudes were shaped by the attribution of his success to opportunities made available in the United States. He did not do well at school (admitting that he had a "C" average) in his country of origin, which prevented him from going to the regional university or to England. Thus he came to the United States to get a university education, and he did exceptionally well, managing to get both an undergraduate degree and a graduate technical and professional degree. Much of his schooling was paid for by scholarship:

> I averaged a 3.4 to a 3.8 GPA and above. That's as an undergrad. From that, each year, I did a little better, applied for different scholarships. I got several of them, so I was able to relieve that burden off my parents as far as having to fund half of my scholarship. I graduated from my undergrad and I got full scholarships to go to graduate school. I averaged the same 3.5, 3.6.

Jason's first impression of the United States was not positive, but he attributes it to his particular experience. He was visiting the country as a member of a sports club, and because they had little money, they were confined to a less desirable part of town. As a result, he was not in a position to understand what the country had to offer.

> So, we came up on this tour. Basically, we were taken to the Bronx. We were put into a hotel. It wasn't—being a small club/organization—it wasn't anything lavish. It was just a small hotel. We were right next to the train station. You lie down at night and you hear the clanging of the trains coming down the train line. Of course, you were introduced—in these motels, they had all the movies. On top of that, the X-rated movies that as a kid, you're like, "OK, let's check it out. Let's see what's going on." Different things. As far as my impression of it, because I was such— I was in such a small, confined area—it was kind of like, "Oh, man, this may not have been all what my uncle and brother made it out to be."

But once he was able to get out of this area, his impression quickly changed. His uncle and brother who lived in the United States introduced him to the real America. Of course, it was an America in which one could retain one's West Indian identity.

> But then after that, when we started actually going to the different areas, being exposed to Van Cortlandt Park, which is this huge park in New York, I mean, it was great. Then you started to see the beauty and stuff of the United States. My uncle, at that time, was also living in Queens. So, I had the opportunity to go and actually visit with him. When I saw the house, the basement, the backyards, all the partying, all the fun stuff that goes on when you have the family reunion in this type of environment, it was kind of like, "OK, this is it. This is a lot of better. It's not what I saw the first time, the first couple of days." I saw the streets were well lit, a lot of trees, very, very wide compared to my country! It's like you can almost take the one and two lanes and combine it and you would say that might be a freeway at home, compared to here. That size

of that road is basically like one and a half lanes. So, those things kind of opened my eyes. I started enjoying it a whole lot more, actually.

While Jason was a student, he spent the summers at his uncle's house. Clearly, his uncle's success and his own educational opportunities reinforced his positive image of the United States and his belief in its desirability. But his cultural roots remained absolutely and unequivocally West Indian. Indeed, his life came to be defined in terms of the dichotomy of culture and success that he defined as the two "types" of West Indians.

Jason's description of West Indian culture is highly exoticized, as evident in his description of West Indian music:

> Our music is fun. It is very sensual or sexually oriented. Just like in reggae, you have reggae and then you have dance hall reggae. It's the same thing—the evolution with calypso/soca. The soca is more like a dance. There's the young people and very fast beat—up tempo—sexual in nature. A lot of waist movements. The calypso is more of a . . . you're not in your head, you're enjoying the music, you're listening to the lyrics, and if you're in a club, you're just chipping and dancing and having a good time all within your self. You're not really carrying on and partying hard, hard, hard, as you would in soca music.

At the same time, he demonstrates this music's similarities to other forms. In the West Indies,

> you also have the other type of music that's political in nature. Calypso music started more as an avenue for people to express themselves, politically. Now, that has changed over the years where we've gone into a different type of music called soca. It's almost similar to like . . . how should I say . . . the rap music, when you have all these different types of rap music right now.

Jason's focus on the similarities among cultural forms in his own background and those other immigrant ethnocultural communities is consistent with how he understands his role as a cultural promoter. His background has enabled his cross-cultural understanding, which is particularly well suited to his agency in bridging the cross-cultural divide. Jason was at pains to point out the cultural heterogeneity of his own country of origin, making him an ideal bridging agent among the many ethnocultural groupings in the Bay Area. He sees himself almost as a promoter of racial harmony in the United States, as someone with the ability to bridge the racial divide: "We came from a different background. We're—we basically grew up with whites, blacks, Syrians, Chinese. It's like, as we call my homeland, it's like a melting pot for all races." Such a background makes him especially suited to the multicultural and multiethnic environment of California and ideally located to mediate between immigrants and "Americans." Thus, his West Indian identity becomes functional in a social arena where the complexities of difference need to be managed.

Jason links his West Indian identity with those of other immigrant communities in the Bay Area, emphasizing the cultural characteristics that he shares with these other immigrant groups. Most important in this regard are the values that he feels "Americans" should adopt. One is "respect for elders. I think [West Indians] in the U.S. here and same is as I've seen in the Chinese culture, the Japanese, the Indian culture, there is a higher degree of respect for the elderly, versus the cultures here in the U.S."

Jason chooses to concentrate on the possibilities for ethnocultural and racial harmony in the United States. He does not see race as a problem except when extraneous factors become intrusive. Indeed, he claimed never to have experienced any racial antipathy:

> When it comes to race, I'm a bit on the naive side. I try to block it out. I don't really look for it. I don't think about it. I have seen. I have heard, but I don't spend that much time worrying about it because all it does, it just basically keeps you back. I am not into allowing someone else to dictate my life, what I should and should not do. I don't know if I can say I put on my blinders, but I really don't look for it.

Jason does not see race as intruding on relations between West Indians, on the one hand, and Latinos and Asians, on the other. Rather, he attributes to economic differences the problems between these groups and African Americans: "I don't think there is any main personality, any major differences because I think the biggest thing that I see is the competition for resources. Resources that are available to foreign nationals."

In Jason's self-conceptualization, it is his role as cultural bridging agent that explains his presence in the United States and his success. He received a higher education because of his university's desire to promote soccer and his own role in its efforts to do so. The opportunity to come to the United States was provided by a soccer scholarship: "The school was looking to promote soccer at the time." In fact, he was both a player and a coach at his university, and he understands soccer to be, ideally, multicultural, and it also represents one of his links with American society as an agent for cross-cultural understanding. Thus his passion for the game has never waned.

> I play a lot of soccer, too. We play against a lot of Latinos in the South Bay Soccer League, who are very competitive because we all believe we have, you know, that we came from an area that has the best style of soccer. That's very competitive from that sport's standpoint. But after it's all said and done, we all have a good time together because we have that common interest, which is in the sport. But as far as anything else, I think we get along pretty decently with a lot of various races.

Jason does not distinguish between soccer and other cultural activities but sees them in almost identical terms. When asked about his efforts to stay in touch with the Caribbean community, he mentioned his role as a distributor of information about soccer:

> It's a combination of involvement with associations, dances. When you go to clubs, you do e-mails—every time I see something—I love soccer— so, every time I see a lot of information about soccer, I send it out to a couple people; call them. It's like, I find out about it, so I jump on the phone, call a couple of people.

Soccer is a metaphor for Jason's role as a cultural promoter. Jason's bacchanalian image of West Indian identity is highlighted in his recounts of his relationship with the community. He describes himself as a "professional partygoer," and so "whenever there is an event, you can be sure that I will be there." He sees this as keeping in touch with the "culture," although his role in cultural promotion began only when he began making cross-cultural connections. He described his exclusive social involvement with the Caribbean community until a few years before the interview. Then, in his words, he began to become involved with Americans: "I started really reaching out. I'm also a bowler. So I bowl. Because that's an American thing, I bowl in leagues during the week. On the weekends, I spend most of my time with the West Indian community." This was the period when his activities began to crystallize around immigrant multiculturalism.

Jason became heavily involved with a group engaged in "the promotion of culture and arts through music. Basically, it's cultures from all over the world, meaning African, Caribbean, and Latin American cultures. That is the basic mission." His explanation for his involvement was that "I just want to do whatever I can to promote the culture."

Jason explained his role in the group as working exclusively "on the Caribbean—which is one of the African Caribbean cultures." He is able to maintain his own distinctive presence and promote his cultural self-images, but in the context of bridging the cultural divide. He characterized the group with which he is involved as diverse: "There's Americans, there's [persons] from India. So, it's a combination of folks. It is more of a melting pot, which I kind of like. It's pretty diverse. It's a lot of fun that way." With this exposure to multiculturalism, he has given up his exclusively West Indian social life: "I can't say right now that I spend most of my time with the West Indians only. But prior to that, it was primarily West Indians. We'd hang out and do this and that. Stuff like that."

Jason's involvement in multicultural promotion escalated rapidly after he attended an event as a member of a West Indian masquerade band, and it evolved into "working with volunteering and stuff like that." At the time of the interview, he "was coordinating the entertainment/hospitality area and was placed in charge of production, the overall production of the festival and coordination of vendors and things like that."

His description of the group's promotional activities matches his self-understanding as a cultural bridging agent. He sees the group as the first

> in the Bay Area to promote the meshing and the blending of calypso and reggae at festivals, and incorporating that with the Brazilian salsa and also the African music. Basically, when you come to the [events], you really have to come with an open mind and just have fun. You will see crafts from around the world. You'll hear music from around the world. You're seeing a melting pot of different races.

But his self-conceptualizations are also those of an ambassador, representing the culture of his identified community to the rest of the world and creating bases for cross-cultural understanding. He thinks of himself as definitely "a Caribbean person, a West Indian person." While he professes his love for all cultures, his cultural being belongs in his homeland: "I love all of the cultures. I love all of the music, all of the different things that the cultures have to offer. However, [I am definitely a West Indian] because I love the music, the food, and all the good stuff." This sentiment is underscored by his refusal to become a citizen of the United States, despite the urging of his friends and family.

And the resistance continues despite the opportunity for dual citizenship. It is clearly an issue with which he is struggling.

> I'm a permanent resident. I have been chastised by friends for years, why haven't I done—as a matter of fact, even last night, why haven't I gone for citizenship because actually as a person from [the West Indies]. I could only speak from that point of view, but we have dual citizenship, where you don't lose anything. I need to go and register to vote and let my voice be heard. For myself, also, but I just haven't done anything. It is something that I have definitely—the intention is there and I think I have made—last night, talking with some friends—I have made that commitment that it's something that I want to have done by mid to late next year. When I say "done," I mean the entire process completed and gotten my citizenship. I have nothing to lose, but it's just procrastination, I guess. A key word, a certain amount of it.

There is no doubt that Jason cannot accept the idea of being an American, which citizenship would symbolize, because it would undermine his role as cultural ambassador and might undermine his own cognitively constructed rationale for being in the United States. One cannot be an ambassador in one's country of citizenship.

Elizabeth Tyler

Those people with a deep longing for the imagined community of their homeland devote themselves to promoting its culture, either to give meaning to their lives in the United States or to reproduce their homeland here. For some, the trauma of immigration is so great that their engagement with the United States becomes minimal, and they perceive everything in America as a reflection of their own experiences at home. Nothing is new, nothing is authentic, and nothing is worthwhile.

Elizabeth Tyler immigrated to the United States in the mid-1980s. She described her family as being extremely poor, insecure, and uncertain. She did not mention a father but only a mother, who worked only sporadically:

> Well, my mom, she worked for a—she used to work—when I first realized who my mom was and recognized my grandmother, she worked in a bar, and she worked in a hotel, and did a couple of different things in my country of origin because the employment situation is not one of such that you have a consistent job. Someday she's working, someday she's

not. I grew up primarily from my grandmother to my mom. And there, of course, was other extended families around.

Despite the social and economic uncertainties, Elizabeth's representations of childhood are happy:

> My childhood was a very happy experience. It was what you would consider for a Third World developing country poor, but it was an enjoyable—not just enjoyable, but the childhood was one of such—it was full of innocence, and it was one that I would want to live again if I possibly could. I remember, it's just a lot of pleasant thoughts.

Perhaps because of her life on the socioeconomic margins, Elizabeth became involved as a teenager with a service club, where she was introduced to cultural performance and offered a way out of social and economic marginalization. The performance and production of popular culture thus became part of her psychological construction of self. She explained that this period was "her time," as if her current existence were in someone else's time:

> I got involved in this [service] club. It's like an after-school program. You go learn to play music. We performed for most of the dignitaries coming to my country. We were playing the hotels. I formed my own dance group. We're talking like the 1970s was my time—that was my time. Not only was I doing the dance group and traveling, I was also an MC, which is here you would call it a mistress of ceremonies, and I would officiate them and announce various events. I had stints on little radio stations there as well, and a lot of personal performing as well. After working in the hotels for a while, I did public relations. I worked as an entertainer. Because of my entertainment background, I worked as an entertainment director at a very early age, which that's like, that doesn't happen.

Then Elizabeth's life seemed to come crashing down when she decided to come to the United States to pursue an education in the entertainment field after enjoying some financial success at a very early age. She almost gave the impression that immigration ended her life: "For a long time, I've been sad, very unhappy. You could call it stop living because a lot of things wasn't in place, wasn't right. Yeah."

At the time of the interview, she had not yet achieved her purpose for being here, and she seemed to blame those who had encouraged her to come to the United States:

Everyone said to me, "God, you have this knack for announcing, for this and that. Why don't you go to school?" And I convinced myself that's what I wanted to do. So I finally decided I had enough money that I wanted to come to America to go to school. So I came to Miami. I was there for a while and was told by friends that it's better to go to California because after a year, you don't have to pay for school. For community college, you don't have to pay. So that was part of why. And I had friends out here in California who—it helped to motivate me to come. They'd say, "Come to California," and I did just that. And then I went to school for a while, and that was that.

There was nothing in America to compensate for her loss of self, which she felt deeply.

When I got to America, at that time, I was an adult. I was like, "This is it?" I remember going to Hollywood on Hollywood Boulevard, and it's like, "Oh, Hollyweird!" [laughs]. I was like, "I've known about this place for a long time." I've always wanted to go back home. I felt—I felt my system, as a person, was not in harmony with my surroundings, with America. They were not in synch. Let me see if I can clarify that. Maybe it's because I'm in love with my country. I'm sorry. It doesn't have all the glitz, the glamour that American has, but call me a patriot, I'm in love with my country. Because it offers me a certain level of feeling—a contentment feeling, a whole feeling, feeling in harmony, the rhythm of who I am in my country. Well, you're born here so maybe that has a lot to do with it. Like here, for whatever reason, I always keep thinking, "I'm going to be going home soon. I'm not even fond of high-rises and all that. To a limit, but some of these super high-rises—I mean, I like to go visit those places. But that's not home. You know, I like the more natural stuff. I like the glitz, the glamour, but I also like a very nice quiet life. Like I can go in my country, I can hang out in the backyard. I can get some coconuts on the coconut tree. See, that is what to me is life. Having all the glitz, the high-rise that is all around me, it's not true living as far as I'm concerned. I'm not totally happy.

It seemed that everything that American had to offer she already had at home. She described her teenaged days as a time that provided her with opportunities to travel:

My childhood also led me to where I was able to travel outside of my country. I remember going to the 1976 Olympics, the 1978 Commonwealth Games. I would go outside of the country and then go back to school because I was still in high school at that time. Just to go. I had friends in some of these countries. They would pay for me, and I would go. That was the kind of childhood.

And America took all that away from Elizabeth. To her, immigration was a step backward:

I'm sure you can understand what I meant—I wish I could have that childhood again. Because the reality is you can't do that now. You can't travel—I traveled so extensively as a child. Now it's the reverse. I can't even go anywhere.

Her memory of her homeland is of urban sophistication. The things that she does here she did as a child in her country of origin. So America has nothing to offer.

I enjoy a vast variety of things. I will enjoy jazz. I'll enjoy different music. I'll go to the theater. I'll go to the opera. I'll do a lot of different things, and I grew up with that around me in my homeland. It's multiracial so you're going to find an intermixing of the nearest cultures, lots of different cultures. So you grew up, I grew up, I won't say well rounded but able to appreciate a wider variety of things. I've always listened to all various kinds of music. They expect me because I'm West Indian, I'm only going to listen to reggae music. On the radio at that point, they'd play Top 40, hear a blend of the southern-state country and western, you hear all these different things coming out of the southern states of America, which we could pick up at home. The radio station at that played a wide variety of music. On a Sunday afternoon, you could be listening to a classic—you could be listening to anything.

Elizabeth reached the same conclusion in her remembrance of the educational system at home:

The educational system was perfect, was wonderful because of what I covered in high school is what college students cover in a year. So when I go to community college here, like some of the stuff, I was having—I remember doing this. I passed it a long time ago. So the educational system in my country—mind you, I have a daughter. I'd love for her to go to school in my country. I would. I really would. So the educational system, as far as I'm concerned, and I will be honest. It's better than here.

Elizabeth considers herself trapped in the United States, as being "tied into the system, and it's kind of hard to pull out to kind of transform yourself and go back. It's not so easy, I think, for a lot of people to do that. Not when you get an apartment and a car, you're paying on a loan. You can't just go."

Since the United States had nothing to offer her and she was trapped, Elizabeth tried to work out her frustrations by attempting to recreate her life back home. This soon came to involve the public production of Caribbean popular culture, Caribbean award shows, Caribbean beauty pageants, and Caribbean fashion shows. She even left her job to start a business doing cultural promotions. Her explanation was that because she had succeeded at home, she could do the same in America. She wanted to show everyone that she could replicate her success.

> I had a full-time job, and I was doing things along the side. I mean, you just hear it all. But I—to be honest, I didn't listen to it. It was like a dare to me. It was like "You're telling me I can't do this? In my country with the resources that I had, I was making money. I was making it happen with their little resources. You're going to tell me that I can't"—it was like a dare sometimes to go out there and just do it, just do it. And then the first year, I just struggled. And then after people started getting comfortable, and they know the quality you put on, then you find people who say, "OK, I like that."

Unlike other West Indian cultural promoters, Elizabeth makes no effort to reach out. She does not see herself as a cultural ambassador. Nor does she try to promote West Indian culture to other cultural communities. She has made very little attempt to reach out even to West Indians from countries other than her own. Rather, she spends her time socializing almost exclusively with persons from her country of origin. It is the sophisticated worldly persona that she sees as being essential to her identity that is not understood by those who are not from her country, and so she avoids them. She explains her nearly exclusive relations with persons from her country of origin in terms of their ability to understand her:

> I think they understand. I think for a large part, they know what I'm about. Because there are more—there are more people like me, and they don't see a lot of—like when I'm out there, they think that everybody is patois, patois, and rolling and laughing, and everybody getting—and most of the time, they don't see me that way, and they don't understand that this is who I was from my country. I didn't come here and be this person who they suppose to be like different. This is who I was from when I can remember myself.

Elizabeth's self-conceptualization strongly associates identity with food. She shops, almost exclusively, at a West Indian market.

> They sell all the staples and all the raw material you need to make any dish you want [from my home]. Green bananas. I love green bananas so I go over there and buy green bananas. Buy cheese because cheese [from home] is different. Everything is just OK, homeward bound. Plantains. I eat a lot of plantains, stuff like that. Oh, God. Dumplings. Salt fish. I cook your typical rice and peas and chicken and aki and saltfish, mackerel. And I get it over there and come home and cook. 'Cause, I don't know, it makes you feel somewhat cultured.

Cultural promotion is the means that Elizabeth uses to ameliorate and manage a life of dislocation and sadness. It keeps her mind off her sense of loss: "I always have to be doing different things to keep my mind going. And especially in America because I don't have family or anything. I find that if I don't do something, I think I'd go crazy."

Conclusion

Cultural promoters emerge in the interstice of the conflict between the popular images and self-representations of West Indians as exotic beings and those of West Indians as being driven by an ethos of success. Those who organize and promote the collectivized West Indian identity in the public arena are the ones who often find themselves on the educational and professional margins. Or they use cultural promotion as a means of identity relocation that is more like a personal journey away from the pollution that comes with being in other sociocultural arenas. Cultural promoters may also see themselves as ambassadors of multiculturalism. In all these interpretations, the single ingredient connecting these people is their longing for an imagined cultural past that they lost when they immigrated. The abstracted memories of their experiences in their countries of origin are combined with cultural images and notions of an idyllic existence. In promoting their culture, they try to reproduce and reclaim their past while seeking opportunities for return. Then, when their cultural promotion brings socioeconomic success, they can use it to explain their continued presence in the United States. At that point, their interests become vested in their host community.

Constructing an identity demands the publicization of collective self-representations, which is what offers opportunities for cultural promotion and legitimizes the role of cultural promoter. Ambivalence toward and ambiguity concerning identity cannot be accommodated. Instead, the role of cultural promotion is reserved for those who can rationalize their reasons to stay. They are the ones whose task it remains to establish the community's presence in the host arena and to define its cultural boundaries.

4

Negotiating the Black-White Dichotomy
Marrying an African American

In this book, I argue that the identities of West Indian middle-class immigrants are negotiated responses to the racialized social order of the United States. They are the means by which West Indians separate themselves from the conceptualizations of American blackness that pervade the popular consciousness. West Indians' understanding of their difference as immigrants is built on notions of foreignness that distinguish between their own values and attributes and those of African Americans. In making these distinctions, West Indians reproduce the schemata of cognitive references that constitute the stereotypes of American blackness. These are combined with tendencies toward the xenophobic rejection of "foreigners" produced by American notions of national superiority and reproduced in the construction of an African American identity. Together, they become the basis for the hostile relationship between the West Indian middle class and African Americans.

African Americans and West Indians do, however, share the experience of being black in America, which forces them into a relationship with each other on the common grounds of racism, racial prejudice, and discrimination and forces on them the need to develop strategies to manage this relationship.

This and the next chapter examine the ways in which West Indians negotiate the black-white dichotomy on both practical and cognitive levels. Marriage between West Indians and African Americans is the subject of this chapter because it demonstrates the challenges of diverse and distinctive understandings of self and the ways in which they are managed. In addition, the intensity and intimacy of marriage give it considerably more urgency while telescoping the problems of difference. The three case studies were chosen for the ways in which they managed fundamental issues of difference. The case studies represent the typical negotiations taking place in the interactions between West Indians and African Americans.

West Indians immigrating to California face a number of obstacles and opportunities which act as filters for the composition of the community and determine patterns of residence and location. Unlike the East Coast, California has no communitywide "West Indian" network that gives immigrants access to social and cultural activities and economic opportunities. West Indians who move to California do so for a number of reasons. Many come to join family or are encouraged by friends to move. Some are transferred by their company. Some are recruited for their skills and education. A few are military personnel who were assigned to California bases and decided to settle in the state after being discharged. Others come seeking professional or high-tech jobs. A few come as students at California universities and colleges. Of the forty-five persons interviewed for this project, twenty-two came to join family members (including spouses or significant others) or to accompany spouses who had been transferred or had secured jobs; thirteen came for education; and nine came seeking better economic opportunities or because they were offered jobs. One even came because of the weather.

This pattern of West Indian immigration to California is consistent with the opportunities available for a secure economic and social presence. These opportunities depend on information available to or contacts made by members of family already established in the state's social economy. Family members can provide access to education and jobs, and they can also provide the means of economic and social survival. Those immigrants without links to family or friends may use the resources of their companies or educational institutions for economic support.

The typical West Indian immigrant to California is in the country legally, even those with family and friends in the state. In fact, West Indians in California are locked out of the "network of social contacts" that give undocumented workers access to unskilled and low-skilled jobs; rather, migrants from Mexico and Latin America dominate these networks. According to a report prepared for the *Los Angeles Times*, "The existence of these networks is a crucial but seldom-discussed reason why poor Latino immigrants seem to have so much more success . . . in finding work" (Goldman 1997:C7). Indeed, so effective are these Latino networks that their use has closed the opportunities for work previously available to the inner-city African American community. This in turn has contributed to an unemployment rate for African Americans in 1997 of 11.5, the highest of any group (Goldman 1997:C7). These networks also limit access to unskilled jobs by West Indians without qualifications and training. In sum, the social and economic viability of undocumented and unskilled West Indians would be seriously jeopardized if they moved to California, as they would have enormous difficulty penetrating the networks that provide access to jobs.

This bias against the undocumented and unskilled was reflected in the composition of the respondents for this study. Three of the forty-five came to California without legal documentation, but two of them almost immediately married a U.S. citizen to secure a legal status. The third, who came to the United States as a student, had a work history and Social Security documentation as a university student, which was enough to hide his undocumented status. Eventually, he also married a U.S. citizen.

The low-skilled, undocumented West Indian immigrant who comes to California without family or friendship ties must rely on the African American community, which cannot always ensure access to social and economic opportunities. Immigrants without such ties who do not match the socioeconomic profile of the West Indian community are forced into lives of social and cultural isolation. In response, some identify themselves as black in order to enter the African American community. They try to find a point of entry that gives their presence some legitimacy and allows them to remain inconspicuous or anonymous. But this ploy can be complicated by unfamiliarity with the subtleties of American blackness. Undocumented West Indians also are usually locked out of the black American networks of family, associations, and friends that stand at the center of the community's survival.

Access to the African American community in California has become even more difficult with the rise of anti-immigrant sentiment, particularly among the working and lower classes. It rose after the recent erosion of African American economic, social, and political power in California, with consequences that have especially affected the lower classes. Because many African Americans attribute this erosion to the influx of immigrants, tensions between the African American and the immigrant communities have worsened. Immigrants are seen to be "taking over," a perception that is supported by the figures. In 1997,

African Americans made up only 7 percent of California's population, compared with 10.9 percent for Asian and Pacific Islanders and 23.2 percent for Hispanics (*California Statistical Abstract* 1999:table B-5). The relative and absolute numbers of the two latter groups are being swelled by immigration. In San Francisco, for example, the African American population fell from 13 percent in 1970 to 11 percent in 1998, and whites, from 46 percent to 38 percent. Between 1990 and 1998, the Asian population increased from 29 percent to 36 percent, and the Latino population rose from 12 percent to 15 percent. These increases have contributed to a significant decline in African American political power (Wagner 2000)

The attitudes of California immigrants, which reflect those of the white community, toward African Americans have contributed to the escalation of tensions. The immigrants feel that African Americans have not properly used the opportunities available to them as U.S. citizens. They compare themselves with African Americans, particularly those in the inner cities who continue to live lives of crime, poverty, and social disarray. Many immigrants cite them as examples of African American inferiority.

African Americans respond with hostility and rejection to the immigrants' attitudes toward them. Their mutual hostilities can be seen in California's politics. In 1994, a state proposition was placed on the ballot to restrict public expenditures for undocumented immigrants, and the campaign for the initiative relied heavily on portraying the immigrants as undesirable. Moreover, even though the initiative was directed at the undocumented, it had implications for the entire immigrant community. The popular representation of immigrants as a drain on public resources struck a resonant chord among the African American lower and working classes, and a substantial majority voted for the initiative, which passed with the support of more than 60 percent of the electorate.

Immigrants complain about what they see as preferential treatment accorded to African Americans. Representatives from the Latino community have charged African Americans with being the "unfair beneficiaries" of jobs in the public sector and attribute their own "underrepresentation" in the public sector to this preference for African Americans (Oliver 1994). Asian Americans complain that affirmative action gives African Americans an unfair advantage in admissions to the state's top public universities, at the expense of their own, "more qualified" children.

Members of the West Indian community in the San Francisco Bay Area hold identical attitudes, and these affect relationships between African Americans and West Indians, particularly when unmitigated by institutional, professional, or historical ties. The problems between African Americans and West Indians are compounded by the particularities of California. On the East Coast, the greatest concentrations of West Indian immigrants live in African American communities, or the two communities exist side by side. The close quarters have fostered a feeling of mutual familiarity and accommodation, if not mutual embrace. In California, however, small numbers and residential dispersion have prevented the development of such familiarity and mutual understanding. Whereas West Indians on the East Coast may find easy entrance into African American society and culture, this is certainly not the case in California. There is no basis for and no history of intermediation. There are no brokers and little need for mutual accommodation and mutual understanding. Without an effective strategy of access, the life of a West Indian in California's African American community can be one of social isolation. The alternative is to become totally immersed in the African American community.

One way that West Indians can enter the African American community is through marriage. But without a history of intermarriage between the two communities, this can be difficult. A few West Indians living in the San Francisco Bay Area have married African Americans. Their marriages and they way they are negotiated shed light on the way the communities understand each other in the Bay Area's sociocultural milieu. Such marriages are particularly problematic among the lower classes but are less so when professional and institutional networks provide alternative means of association and other understandings. In many instances, one of the partners must decide to absorb the cultural frame of reference of the other, or the marriage would collapse.

The following case studies show the possibilities and limitations of marriage between African Americans and West Indian immigrants. Sometimes, mutual understandings emerge from the tensions and hostilities produced by interpersonal conflict. The case studies also reveal the central role of American racial discourse in the formation of a West Indian identity. In sum, for the West Indian middle class, identity as a West Indian is a means of escaping American blackness. But this possibility of escape inevitably introduces hostility and tension into their relationships.

George Clement Bryan

George Bryan is a black man from Guyana, from the lower class, as reflected in his educational, social, and cultural attributes. To improve his economic situation, he immigrated illegally to the United States in 1972 when he was a seaman, remaining in the country after his vessel berthed in Miami.

Bryan initially used the West Indian employment network on the East Coast to work at odd jobs. He was able to support himself and send cash to his mother and sisters in Guyana. They all became quite dependent on him. After spending some time on the East Coast, Bryan decided to go to California, but he had none of the skills that would qualify him for job sponsorship and he had no ties to family and friends in the state. And he was undocumented. So Bryan found himself socially and economically isolated and unable to penetrate the class-specific social network of West Indians in the San Francisco Bay Area. (Since all the information about Bryan used in this account is contained in the public record, I have made no attempt to hide his identity. Some of the information was gathered from personal interviews when I served as an expert witness in a capital case in which he was the accused. As required by the court, all my notes from these interviews became part of the public record.)

Unlike the educated, skilled, and professional classes and those permitted to enter the United States for family reunification, Bryan faced impenetrable barriers to legal migration. Pride and fear of discovery made him afraid to form relationships with other West Indians. He became uncomfortable and cautious and began using someone else's name to hide his illegality. His social status profoundly affected his "attitude." He never felt free to move about and believed that he was being "held back" and had a "ball and chain" hanging on him.

Bryan was living in the inner city of Oakland, California, where he met an African American woman named Barbara. She provided him with access to the socioeconomic network of Oakland's inner-city community and to the social economy of the African American lower class. Despite his misgivings about African Americans, he entered into a romantic relationship for the considerable benefits that it brought. His original intention was to remain in the relationship until he met a "more suitable" partner for marriage. In the interim, Barbara gave him an entrée into African American inner-city life.

Marriage to an American offered Bryan the only means available to him of becoming a legal resident. But Barbara's inner-city mores and lifestyle conflicted sharply with his West Indian sensibilities, and he was reluctant to marry her. With the birth of a child, however, this reluctance vanished, and the couple was married. For Bryan, it was both a moral and a functional decision. He saw the marriage as providing an opportunity to legalize his status. To this were added the strictures of his background and culture against "living together" and having children. In his view, "the baby and the prospect of getting permanent residence were all tied up in one bundle as the reason for marrying."

The cultural and attitudinal differences between Bryan and his wife created an extremely volatile relationship. The hostility and distrust from their cross-cultural prejudices and stereotypes soon began to intrude into Bryan's relationship with Barbara's family. There were no brokers and mediators with cross-cultural understandings to introduce Bryan and his wife to the ways and practices of each other's culture. There was no history of cultural hybridization that would provide a space for mutual understanding. Rather, the intimate connection that the two maintained with their families only reinforced their misunderstandings.

Bryan remained in frequent contact with his mother and sisters in Guyana through phone calls and letters. He discussed with them all the details of his and his wife's relationship, and they responded from the perspective of their own sociocultural values. The ties to his family in Guyana were reinforced by their growing economic dependence on the money that he sent back to them, and they began to develop a stake in his marriage. This stake guaranteed his security and stability and ensured his further assistance. Moreover, it held out the possibility that they could immigrate under the terms of family reunification.

Bryan saw his wife's welfare-dependent background as confirming his own understanding of African Americans as lazy and immoral. He also saw African American immorality in his wife's sense of independence and her refusal to submit to his will. He complained to his family that he had little control over her behavior. Her impertinence conflicted with his notions of male authority and female subservience.. He was both unable and unwilling to countenance her refusal to concede to his authority.

As this hostility toward his wife and her family escalated, Bryan increasingly turned to his mother and sisters back home for emotional support. They in turn reconfirmed his culturally rooted expectations of spousal behavior. They saw his "manhood" as impugned and constantly pointed out to him his need to reassert it. They began to insist that he take measures to ensure that Barbara's behavior comported with the expectations of "reputation" and "respectability" imposed on black lower-class wives throughout the West Indies (see Yelvington 1995). But these culturally rooted expectations conflicted with the more equalitarian ethos of marital relationships in the United States. The conflict applied particularly to the social, economic, and cultural contexts of gender relations in black inner-city communities. Although his wife's socialization in such a community produced fundamentally different expectations in the marital relationship, Bryan interpreted her behavior as deviant and immoral. He objected to a lifestyle that included drinking alcohol and "partying" with the "socially undesirable," a term that he probably applied to most African American inner-city residents. He saw Barbara's behavior as responsible for the neglect of household duties that, from his cultural perspective, were exclusively hers to perform. He was particularly incensed over what he saw as a dereliction of her role as a mother to their daughter. And he despised her decision to remain on welfare even after they were married. This was a source of considerable embarrassment, since it involved his family in the type of immorality and laziness that he attributed to the African American character.

Bryan saw his wife's moral character reflected in her attitude toward self-improvement. He believed that she had no motivation, and he expressed amazement at her decision not to make use of her high-school diploma. In this, he was ignorant of the realities of racism and discrimination and their effects on the African American inner-city community. Instead, he believed that a high-school diploma, which he did not have, was the route to success and prosperity. He constantly encouraged Barbara to enter nursing school, which she refused to do. And he lamented her tendency to seek employment in minimum-wage occupations, whenever she did decide to work. Bryan also had practical concerns. He saw Barbara's absence of motivation, determination, ambition, and perseverance as directly affecting his own chances for improvement and as directly responsible for the family's continued economic marginality. Barbara had the means for the kind of achievement that would give the family the status expected of West Indians in the Bay Area.

Barbara's unemployment, dependence on welfare, and low income hurt Bryan's aspirations for himself and his family at home hoping to immigrate. Her dependence on welfare jeopardized his chances for acquiring legal immigrant status as a permanent resident, as it was normally used by the U.S. Immigration and Naturalization Service as an indication of financial insecurity. As a result, Barbara could not meet the required criteria of financial support, which made her ineligible to act as Bryan's sponsor for legal status.

All these factors deepened Bryan's frustration and his insecurity and led to physical abuse. Naturally, Barbara's family came to her defense, which added to Bryan's social isolation and his sense of his loss of manhood. It also intensified his emotional dependence on his family back home. Likewise, his wife turned more and more to her Oakland family for emotional support. They began seeing in Bryan's behavior manifestations of his foreignness. As family became more involved, they reinforced the values feeding the negative stereotypes that had become bases of understanding in the marriage. Barbara's family considered Bryan to be "uncivilized," and they began threatening to report his physical abuse to the authorities and to use it as grounds for deportation. This confirmed Bryan's growing suspicion that Barbara's family was bent on jeopardizing any possibility of his winning legal immigrant status. Some members of her family began to use violence against him whenever he became abusive toward her, which became a source of persistent humiliation. From his cultural perspective, it was an attack on his manhood.

Bryan's humiliation, fears, and insecurity combined to reinforce his social isolation. His undocumented status made him uncomfortable and prevented him from establishing social ties outside the home. This, from his perspective, left no one to represent "his side" and to intervene on his behalf in his dispute with his wife and her family. He became convinced that members of his wife's family were the source of his marital problems. So Bryan began urging her to break her ties with them, referring to them as "devils."

When Bryan's efforts to "reform" his wife failed, he thought about divorcing her. But he quickly recognized its drawbacks. Divorce would magnify his problems, since he depended on his wife's welfare payments and her income from her odd jobs. More important, divorce would end whatever chance he still had of securing legal permanent residence. It was not simply a matter of leaving his wife and setting out on his own. For all these reasons, he made an attempt at reconciliation, based on Barbara's willingness to sever her ties to her family. But Barbara refused and, instead, left home. Bryan was terrified at the prospect of having to return to his homeland as a deportee with "only the shirt on his back" after spending fourteen years in the United States. He would return without money or qualifications and be subjected to ridicule. His family would suffer shame and disappointment. He saw it as a fate worse than death.

Bryan's frustrations and fears intensified when he could not find his passport. He convinced himself that his wife's family had taken it as part of their plan to get him deported. He was certain that they were about to report him to the Immigration and Naturalization Service. Accordingly, in July 1983, in a fit of desperation and rage, he bought a rifle, which he used to murder his wife, her mother, and her sister. For this crime, he was sentenced to life without the possibility of parole.

Bryan's case study is an extreme example of the frustrations produced by social isolation. He had moved to California without the support of family and the means to secure a stable existence. His cultural frame of reference was reinforced by the strong ties that he maintained with his family in Guyana. The West Indian community in the Bay Area and the inner-city African American community occupied different social locations, with no history of interaction between them and no history of social practices to serve as a bridge between them. Bryan and his wife were brought together under circumstances that only exacerbated their stereotypical judgments about each other and that were reinforced by their bonds with their own families.

Bryan's social isolation was produced in the context of a collective conscience of West Indian achievement. He could not "belong" to the Bay Area's West Indian community because of his illegal and low socioeconomic status. Unlike the cultural promoters, he was unable to develop alternative means of entry. Unlike West Indians in the military, he had no institutional bases of absorption into the American ethos. And unlike West Indians in New York, there were no bridging mechanisms to promote mutual understandings between the African American and West Indian identific communities. West Indian antipathy to African Americans and their hostility toward "foreigners" were reinforced in Bryan's relationship with his wife. There were no possibilities for amelioration. If his wife rejected her African American past, Bryan would have no welcoming community to which her identific allegiance could be transferred, unlike many other African American spouses of West Indians. So the only alternative was separation. Isolation and marginalization had left Bryan without the option of entering the West Indian community. His sense of permanent foreignness would have been violated if he returned to Guyana. He was left in a state of anomie.

Peter Lashley

Education, socioeconomic status, and a willingness and desire to become immersed in the social culture of one's partner can mitigate and even remove the tensions and volatility in intimate relationships between West Indians and African Americans.

Peter Lashley immigrated to California from the West Indies in the early 1980s. (This and all subsequent names are fictitious to protect the author's identity. Details that could identify the respondent also have been changed. The data are from a formal tape-recorded interview and several informal discussions with the respondent.) Peter arrived with a high-school education and training in accounting and finance. Before immigrating, Peter had worked as a primary-school teacher, and then he got a job as a semiprofessional in the accounts division of one of the largest companies in his home country. His education and occupation before immigrating placed him at the upper end of the lower middle class. His extended family stretched from working class to upper middle class. It was a typically upwardly mobile Caribbean family.

Peter's brother had immigrated to the United States in the early 1970s and had joined the U.S. military to become a legal resident and to obtain more education. While enlisted, he managed to complete an undergraduate degree. Then after an honorable discharge, he used the benefits of the GI bill to earn a graduate degree in a professional field. He lived in the San Francisco Bay Area during his enlistment. Peter's brother had become active in the African American community during his enlistment. Although he continued to identify with it after his discharge, his involvement with West Indians now was confined to playing the game of cricket. Otherwise, he presented himself as African American and hid his West Indian background. As soon as he became a U.S. citizen, he sponsored the immigration of his mother and Peter as permanent residents.

Peter decided to join his brother in California and, in the absence of an alternative, first developed social ties with the African Americans with whom he began to fraternize. He did not know a West Indian community even existed. Peter found a relatively low level job in a major financial firm, as a stepping-stone to a better job.

> I was single. So I was pretty much focused in terms of just trying to get better in my job. In terms of what I experienced over there, I think it kind of made me want—once you started working your first job, and you have certain goals in mind, I think you put your best foot forward, and I think that's basically what I did. I just tried to make the best out of the job that I had to try and make my promotional opportunities as good as they can be.

Peter's attitude, while characteristic of the self-understandings of achievement held by West Indians in the Bay Area, was forged in the middle-class ethos of his country of origin, but it had little to do with the construction of West Indian identity in the Bay Area. Nonetheless, Peter quickly began to move up the occupational ladder through hard work and the skills that he had acquired at home. He upgraded these skills by taking targeted college courses and on-the-job training.

Peter entered the East Bay African American community through his brother's network. He was able to secure a semiprofessional job in his field and move up the occupational ladder. Besides the financial security of a job, he was able to share in the economic and social stability established by his brother, with whom he lived. As Peter became more independent and informed, however, he found his way into the West Indian community. Unlike Bryan, his socioeconomic status enabled his easy absorption into the community and its activities and associations with which he soon became involved.

Although Peter's brother had provided Peter with an introduction to the African American community, Peter's entry was not supported by a history of prior insertion, so it did not come with the feeling of comfort and normalcy enjoyed by his brother. Peter therefore began to distance himself from his brother's social network, using his brother's marriage to an African American woman as an excuse to set out on his own. He rented a house with a cousin who was active in the affairs of the West Indian community.

Peter met and married an African American professional who had become involved with the West Indian community. Together, they bought a home and had several children. After their marriage, his wife's relationship with the West Indian community intensified, although she maintained close relations with her parents, her siblings, and a few close African American friends whom she introduced to her West Indian social circle. But her social life was centered in the West Indian community. She acquired a West Indian accent and became familiar with the nuances of Peter's cultural background.

Apart from relations with his in-laws and his professional on-the-job affiliations, Peter's and his wife's associations were confined to the Bay Area's West Indian social network. He rarely saw or communicated with his brother, who continued his involvement with the African American community. Peter, however, tried to reproduce the social and cultural conditions of the life he had enjoyed before immigrating. He identified himself as a "black West Indian" and distinguished himself from "African Americans." His reason for having nothing in common with African Americans was, he declared, that "maybe I feel that I'm better than a black American. It's just the way I am. It's who I am."

In other words, Peter was as uncompromisingly West Indian as Bryan was, as reflected in every aspect of his social and cultural life and in his associational and friendship ties. After seventeen years in the United States at the time of the interview, Peter still refused to become a citizen because "I think deep down inside, I think I would like to see myself going back to my country under the right circumstances and maybe living in my country." His West Indian—foreign—identity dictated his choice of activities: "I play cricket, and that's part of my culture that I can't ever let go. I have to play cricket, not soccer. Cricket. That is—that is part of—by playing cricket, that also enables me to hold onto some of my culture in the sense of some of the sports that we really get involved in back home." He went exclusively to "Caribbean clubs" because "with anything back home that I miss, you know, I try to get involved in anything that's happening within the Caribbean." He ate West Indian food "all the time" because "that part of my culture I don't think will ever go away. I still have the West Indian food. I eat rice every day. It's just part of me." In other words, he saw his West Indian identity in essentialist terms.

And yet he remained happily married to an African American woman because of the bridges that each was able to build with the host community of the other. Both came to the marriage already familiar with each other's social-cultural background. Peter's exclusive relationship with the African American community before his introduction to the West Indian sociocultural network had provided exposure, familiarity, and understanding. Even though he had severed these ties, they served as the basis of understanding and respect in his marriage, despite the almost identical views of African Americans that he shared with Bryan. One example is his opinion about what Peter considered to be the welfare dependency of African Americans. Whereas Bryan's stereotypical views were reinforced and confirmed by his wife and her family, Peter was married to a college-educated professional from the African American middle class. Her parents also were professionals, contradicting his own stereotypes. Rather, his earlier experience with African Americans provided a context for explaining what he saw as their dependence on the welfare state. For this reason, his views had been tempered, even though they were equally stereotypical:

> The welfare system I personally basically think was designed to primarily keep African Americans within that system where they become dependent on the welfare system or like that. A lot of them have grown up in that system, and it's very difficult for them to get out of it. So that's why you find that instead of them basically—why should they go work a job that they may consider as menial when they could basically go to a welfare line and probably get a fair amount of money?

Peter's views of African Americans as a whole were similarly contextualized. What he considered to be an African American social and moral crisis he saw as quite pervasive. But he located the source of the problem in the social system in which African Americans were forced to live. Unlike Bryan, he did not see it as an essentialized, inherent trait. Instead, the system explained the African American failure to achieve. Peter was clearly uncomfortable explaining his views of African Americans, particularly in the presence of his wife, who was listening to the entire interview. But he was not deterred from offering his opinions:

> Well, I just think personally I think African Americans, I just think due to the fact that they've been in what is considered a system whereby things have been pretty rough in African Americans in the sense of where it's come to—what job opportunities, basically just living, I think I would say on the average a lot of black Americans bought into the system in the sense that they're contributing to it, and not trying to make things better for themselves. I think as the years progress, we're finding more and more black Americans are definitely trying to make a difference with their personal lives, with their family lives, but still I think too much of, too much of a percentage of the black Americans are still contributing to the system that basically makes it difficult for blacks to succeed.

Contributing in the sense that they are not really looking for opportunities to better themselves.

In other words, Peter's view of African Americans is somewhat flexible. Because he believes some African Americans are "trying to make a difference," this opens the way for accommodation. His wife's social and educational background clearly placed her among those who are "making a difference with their personal lives, with their family lives."

Peter sees his American-born family as his link to the United States, unlike Bryan, who saw his wife and her family as a morally corrupting influence on their only child. Bryan became obsessed with protecting his daughter from the "evil influences" of his wife's family, and while incarcerated, he waged a legal battle to gain custody of his daughter and have her sent back home into the care of his mother and his siblings. Peter, however, was able to distinguish between what he considered "home" and his identity. Home, for him, was the location of his family, and all the members of his nuclear family were Americans: "Home for me right now is in California because my family is here. My immediate family is here. Most of my relatives are in the United States, but for me personally, right now, home is in California." He accepted this despite serious misgivings, such as that America might culturally pollute his children. So he made his declaration of "home" with considerable apprehension:

> Well, still, even though I consider California home, I think it's for the benefit of my kids, I think I would like them to basically get involved with—actually I would prefer to have them grow up where I came from, to be honest with you, for the schooling because I think it would just make them think better for them. I think they would have a different view in terms of what life is all about, and I think their focus would be different.

But Peter accepted that America was where they belonged:

> They grew up in America, so like that, it would be—I guess my job would be pretty difficult in terms of—what I try to instill my values in terms of the way I grew up, but still I think the bottom line is the environment in which—that surrounds them, it makes it much more difficult. You try to instill your values, and you try to do as best as you can with the kids, but it does help if the surrounding environment basically is the same in terms of what you're trying to instill in your kids. Home is California. I wouldn't send them home unless me and my wife were there,

and my wife is from America, and so it would—for her, I would also have to think in terms of my wife. She is an American so that would make it difficult. First of all, my wife would have to like being in my country before I even considered basically taking the kids back there.

Clearly, the class position of Peter's wife and her role as a bridge to the wider society as a whole, particularly as an African American, reduced the possibility of culturally rooted conflict. Their social and economic dependence on each other supported the lifestyle that Peter had anticipated when he immigrated to the United States. They were able to live the West Indian middle-class ideal without Peter's having to compromise his West Indian identity. His wife acted as a link to American society and the benefits that it could provide. At the same time, he did not depend on her for his economic and social well-being. Her willingness to "give up" her American identity and to share his identific participation in the West Indian community minimized the kind of culture clash that Bryan constantly experienced with such tragic consequences.

The representations and practices of West Indian identity in the San Francisco Bay Area helped Peter's and his wife's successful negotiation of difference. When he met his wife, Peter was not in the best social and economic position to win approval from her family. And indeed, they disapproved of him as her future husband. He did not have a university education and had only just begun to move up in his company. In the eyes of his wife's middle-class African American parents, his family of origin did not appear to be socially and culturally "appropriate" and worthy of their daughter. Peter played a central role in a social network of younger West Indians because of his participation in West Indian sports. He hosted many gatherings of the group of younger West Indian males at his home. There was always music, alcohol, and West Indian food (usually prepared by Peter himself). These activities were accompanied by the rambunctiousness usually associated with young men, exaggerated by typical West Indian boisterousness. To the jaundiced eye of his wife's middle-class family, these were like the gatherings of young men in African American inner cities, complete with images of drugs, crime, and gangs. It certainly did not look good for their daughter's future. It also did not help that Peter and his wife were living in an apartment in a working-class neighborhood.

In reality, however, most of those who gathered at Peter's home were themselves quite successful, highly educated, and in well-paid occupations. Initially, his in-laws were unable to read the social and economic cues of the West Indian community, but Peter's wife could. Because she recognized that her parents' understanding was wrong, she was able to withstand the brunt of their criticism. And as Peter moved up the socioeconomic ladder and with the birth of children, they became more familiar with West Indian customs and Peter's friends.

Peter began to acquire the trappings of a successful middle-class lifestyle, including a home in the suburbs. This and his demonstrated commitment to family, promotion, success, reputation, responsibility, and a comfortable life was precisely what his wife's parents had hoped for in a son-in-law. So the barriers to cross-cultural understanding were shattered, and a mutual understanding was forged in the commonality of the middle-class ethos of Peter's West Indianness and his in-laws' socioeconomic status.

The basis for this development was the construction of a West Indian identity in California. It made Peter's "foreignness" acceptable because of its orientation toward achievement and success. His West Indian identity, reflecting the representations and practices of the Bay Area's West Indian community as a whole, explained the insulation of his marriage from the initial negative pressures of his in-laws. The fundamental about-face in their attitude toward Peter emerged when they understood his identity. The change was from hostility and rejection to admiration, respect, and support.

Jane Peters

Sometimes a marriage between a West Indian and an African American is successful despite social and cultural isolation from the West Indian community and rejection of an African American identity and affinity by the West Indian spouse. Instead, location in a socially and culturally neutral environment can provide an opportunity to manage difference.

Jane Peters left her country of birth in the early 1950s after the death of her parents and estrangement from her siblings. Her roots lay in the upper echelons of her country's color hierarchy and in its middle socioeconomic stratum. The expectations of her position meant that she should marry someone in the upper socioeconomic bracket of her country. But these expectations were frustrated when in her late teens, Jane gave birth to a child out of wedlock. Forced to leave the country to avoid the consequences of a tarnished reputation and a loss of respect, she had few skills when she moved to Europe. While there, Jane was forced to work in a number of low-skilled occupations, and she failed in her attempt at training in a subprofessional field. Then she met and married an African American military serviceman stationed in Europe. They lived there until he was transferred to the midwestern United States. After four years, he was reassigned to another of America's European bases. In 1965, her husband was transferred to a military base in Northern California, and ever since then, they have lived just outside the San Francisco Bay Area.

While living in California, Jane managed to obtain a relatively high paying job. Her husband's military benefits and a good job after retiring from the military have combined with hers to support a materially comfortable life. Her husband was continuing to work at the time of the interview, although Jane had decided a few years earlier to remain at home.

Like Bryan and Peter, Jane has maintained a strong West Indian identity. She continues to speak with a strong West Indian creole accent even after being away from her country of origin for forty-two years. Since leaving in 1950, she returned home for the first time only in 1988. But she maintained a strong sense of West Indianness despite her isolation and separation from West Indians and the West Indian community. In fact, she has had very little contact with West Indians after leaving Europe in 1960. Despite separation from her "roots" and the long absence from her home, she has continued to identify with her country of origin: "It is where my heart is. That's where my navel string is buried. My heart is there also." This identity does not come without equivocation:

> I have two homes. When I'm in my country, when I go on vacation, I'm itching to get back here. And when I'm here, I long to go home. So I'm in-between. And they're pulling and tugging. But I dream—when I dream, it's just about my country of origin. I love that place.

The circumstances under which Jane and her husband met were highly conducive to a successful marriage, despite the absence of bridging experiences that help explain Peter's successful marriage and those marriages in locations like New York with histories of intercultural contact between African Americans and West Indians. Rather, when Jane and her husband first met, they shared their foreignness and their race, which enabled them to bond with each other. Their support for each other in social and cultural environments that had little in common with their own was the dominant feature of their entire life together. Each became the other's pillar of support in the face of the racial hostilities that they have had to endure throughout their lives.

When they met, they both were black foreigners living in Europe and considered "different." In this context both were psychologically and emotionally prepared to negotiate their own sociocultural "differences," and so they did not loom large, as they did with Bryan and his wife. They developed a strong bond centered on themselves and their family, which Jane frequently emphasized in the interview: "Sometimes I want privacy with my husband. I don't like too many people hanging around me. Maybe that's why I am by myself, you understand? I don't like to share my husband or my family with nobody. I'm jealous though."

Unlike Bryan, Jane and her husband found themselves far away from family and neighbors and the social network that each had left at home. Neither lived in an identific community that reinforced popularly held stereotypical understandings about the other, as did Bryan. And this circumstance continued throughout their marriage. Jane's husband never returned to his community of origin, nor did he maintain close relationships with his own family.

While Jane and her husband bonded together against the outside world, each managed to create a space to exercise their personal independence. For Jane's husband, this space was provided by the military and, after his discharge, by a job that shared many of the features of military life. Jane also sought independence through the several jobs that she had held throughout her life. She "worked in different places on the base, you know, like in the Apex, doing inventory and stuff like that. All those things I never really liked. I did maid work. I did all kinds of work. As long as it was honest, I worked." She attributes her predisposition to hard work to her West Indianness.

When she moved to California, Jane was not content to have only one job: "I used to leave one [job] and go to one in another county. And they used to give me an hour in between to get there. I used to go almost sixteen hours a day in fact." She saw her jobs as giving her economic independence:

I like money. I really do. Not to say I like money that I'm greedy. I like money because if I want something, I'll get it, OK. It's not like I can't get it from my husband. I can get it from my husband, but I like my own stuff. So when I spend it, nobody can say, "Why are you spending so much?" It's mine.

Their independent lifestyles have allowed Jane and her husband to retain the cultural integrity of their origins. Unlike Peter's wife, neither has been forced to adopt the culture of the other. Jane sees herself and her husband as being on different "sides" of a cultural divide. This was evident in her answer about her children's identity: "They take both sides. At times, they like my side a little bit more [laughs] than they like their father's. And then they like their father's at times more than they like mine."

Jane and her husband have maintained the bond between them because both have remained free from the social network of influences of their families and communities of origin. They have not developed any strong relationships with either African Americans or West Indians. Jane claimed to have no African American friends:

> I don't socialize very well. And I adjust to that because some of them say things, and I do not like to hear them say what they say, you know. Because if you can bring one, you can carry one. That's my philosophy, and I don't have time for that. I love to read. I love to walk. I love to do a lot of things that people don't like to do. They like to party, drink, get drunk. I don't do that. I'm a stay homebody. That's me. And I don't put no hat higher than I could reach. I ain't taking no stick to take a dump.

Jane has not developed relationships with West Indians either: "There's not that many around here. They live too far for me to visit. I don't drive out of town anymore."

It is interesting that the one close friendship that Jane and her husband developed in the Bay Area was with a family identical to their own in many respects. Jane's husband met a fellow serviceman who was from her country of origin, and he also was married to an African American. These shared circumstances led to the establishment of a strong bond. Despite the differences in their ages, the two families became extremely close.

Jane used her friendship with the young family to reestablish contact with her roots. She and her husband were introduced by their friends to a few other West Indian families whom they would occasionally invite to their home. They renewed her interest in her homeland. In the late 1980s, Jane contacted her family back home and went back in 1988 to attend her brother's funeral. It was her husband's first visit to her country of origin and the first time that she had returned in thirty-eight years. Their visit led to the development of a new phase in their lives. Jane and her husband began making frequent visits home and hosting small groups of West Indians to look at videotapes of the visits and to listen to the latest in music from her homeland. Jane also used these occasions to cook West Indian dishes.

Jane's husband was enthusiastic about her efforts to rekindle ties to her family and culture. Soon her brothers and their family began visiting her in California. For the first time in their marriage, they were connected with family. At the same time, Jane is careful to acknowledge her husband's African American identity. She does not force her own West Indianness on him and makes sure that he has the opportunity for his own identific self-expression. This was evident when they began to consider settling in her country of origin. She recognized that her husband might also want to reestablish ties to his own roots: "My husband and I were going to buy a house over there when he retires. This is the second job he's going to retire from. And then he's going to buy [a house] in Denver and go every six months to and from both of them."

The success of their marriage clearly rests on Jane's willingness and ability to accommodate the differences between her own West Indian origin and her husband's African American origin. They also were able to insulate themselves from the social forces that might have destroyed their relationship. Their isolation from the African American community minimized the consequences of the negative stereotypes of African Americans that Jane continued to harbor. Her dislike for African Americans was intense because "they always think that we've come over here to take the money. And every time they tell me that, I say, 'Exactly. You don't like to go to school, and you don't like to work. So I'll come, and I'll take it.' They don't really like me."

Jane thinks of her family as a unit and everyone else as an outsider, thereby exempting her husband from her negative opinion of African Americans. Despite reestablishing contact, Jane continued to think of her family as outsiders. She describes herself as having "nobody. See, my sister had a family. She takes care of herself. My brother had his own family. So all of them had their own lives."

The social and cultural arena provided by the San Francisco Bay Area was ideally suited to accommodate the negotiated realities of Jane's marital life. Her middle-class life in the California suburbs permitted the self-representation of her "foreignness" and her sense of difference from African Americans. It also allowed her to avoid associating with African Americans, whom she disliked because of her perception that they were hostile to those who were different:

> Some black Americans when I first came here, we were living in the apartments. I said good morning to some black people, and they looked at me, and just turned their heads and just keep on walking. I guess because of my color, you know. They don't like yellow people or yellow niggers or red niggers or whatever they call us. But they wouldn't even talk. That's why I stay by myself. I associate myself with some people and with some people I don't.

Social separation from the African American community eliminated the tensions that emerge when conflict-producing values are reinforced by cultural contact. Jane's husband's participation in the African American social and cultural network might have led to such reinforcement, and it might also have exposed Jane to conflicts in her relations with her husband's community.

The dispersion of the West Indian community was also culturally insulating, as it permitted Jane to negotiate her identity outside the dictates of the West Indian community. Indeed, she had to seek out West Indians, for there was no residential community to attract her participation, no pervasive presence of West Indians to make her association with them unavoidable. Thus, Jane remained free to define herself in ways that accommodated her husband's sensibilities.

Conclusion

These three case studies highlight the major issues of West Indian identity construction in the United States. West Indians and African Americans are forced into relationships with each other on the basis of their shared blackness and their histories of participatory experiences. West Indians use popular understandings of their exoticized foreignness to distinguish them from popular concepts of American blackness. These distinctions are compounded by the absence of a historical framework for understanding and participating in the African American community. The case study of Bryan shows how these distinctions can combine to produce friction between the two groups.

Without any way of reducing this conflict, these relations can have violent outcomes.

California's social geography is not conducive to the development of bridging mechanisms for accommodating the differences between the two communities. Rather, the possibilities for coming together based on the shared element of blackness are limited, at best, which explains the intensification of mutual hostilities that eventually led to Bryan's murder of his wife, her sister, and her mother.

Peter Lashley's case study demonstrates how the common aspirations of the West Indian and African American middle and professional classes can mitigate the negative implications of their different self-conceptualizations. Once class distinctions are eliminated, West Indian and African American high achievers look surprisingly alike, even in their rejection of African American lower-class practices. Common aspirations can become the bases for successful and productive relations even in the face of mutually held prejudices against each other's communities.

The case study of Jane Peters points out the shared element of blackness and the bond that it can create between members of the two communities when they unite against a racially hostile world. This unity can be maintained even when the negative views of the other linger. The union of Jane and her husband was maintained apart from each other's identific communities, and it insulated them from the influences that could have reinforced negative stereotypes of each other and led to hostility and violence. This is what occurred in Bryan's case.

5

Negotiating the Black-White Dichotomy
Images of African Americans

In the discourse of difference, West Indians' identific construction in California has two central elements: their blackness and their status as immigrants. Each has certain ambiguities. On the one hand, blackness gives West Indians a particular "claim" to the legitimacy of belonging, which translates into access to resources as "blacks." That is, it links West Indians to the political and social agendas of African Americans. Blackness also allows West Indians the opportunity to be apolitical as a group, relying on the social and political agency of the African American community to protect their civil rights and to contest racialized barriers to success.

The social construction of the West Indian immigrant identity functions as a foil against white racial exclusionary practices and the generalized practices of white racial aversion to African Americans. It emerges out of exoticized self-representations that constitute the cognitively constructed reflexive gaze of whites. It is the panoptic vision of the West Indian that exists in the tourist imagination. This socially constructed understanding allows West Indians in California to carve out a space within the group of immigrants identified as high achievers. Their very "foreignness," derived from the popular images of them, protects West Indians from the taint of blackness as they negotiate the racialized domain of American discourse of difference.

These are the ambiguities in the representations and practices of West Indian immigrants in the Bay Area. Each immigrant has his or her own history of participatory experiences, which adds to the identific construction. Identity includes the symbolic choices of association. The people with whom one associates and the nature and content of associational behavior are part of the process of identific construction.

Within the broad contours of West Indian identity, each person uses a set of constantly changing strategies to negotiate the American racialized identity.

Bridget Barlow

A Caribbean identity is available as an escape from the repressive conditions of blackness pertaining to African American identific construction. West Indians can become "Americanized" when they enter into geosocial arenas where the construction of identity is organized around ethnicized understandings of Americanness. This process of reproduction is typical of West Indian identity discourses on the East Coast, especially among West Indians in New York City. These ethnicized constructions can cause the African American identity to be internalized. The agency, legitimacy of belonging, and symbolic power of African Americans may be attractive when negotiating social location in American sociocultural and political space. But they come with the heavy burden of American racism. West Indians who become racialized African Americans are quickly sensitized to the limitations of race imposed by the systemic organization of difference. One way in which these limitations may be handled cognitively and practically is to escape American definitions of self altogether. For immigrants, this may mean reasserting their West Indian identity.

Bridget Barlow arrived in the United States when she was eight years old. She came to join her parents, who had left her behind to live with her grandmother. She moved to Brooklyn in 1968 at the beginning of the post-1965 influx of immigrants produced by changes in the immigration statutes. It was a period when the West Indian community was not well defined. Bridget remembers that "there were a lot of Irish around. We're talking poor people here, so there are Irish, and then you have the West Indians and the black Americans. Different types of people but probably a lower class of people in the Brooklyn area." This produced considerable pressure on her to be "American." Bridget was particularly conscious of her "difference":

> My father was very West Indian and my stepmother. But very West Indian to where I didn't want my friends to come over because his accent annoyed me. But I was trying so desperately to mesh with the Americans because it's peer pressure at the age when I came into. So that's what I

had to deal with. I'm dealing with kids that laugh at me because one, I had an accent. And laugh at me because I wore a natural with a part in it, which nobody else did, but my father combed my hair so I looked like a boy, and I wore Jim boots, which nobody else did. And I was thin and tall. I was probably the tallest girl in the class at the time. At that point, I was the tallest girl. So those were my disappointments, were that kids weren't friendly. It took a long time to really be a part. To be accepted by the American kids, and I went to school with a lot of white kids.

Bridget emphasized, however, that she wanted to be "American," and her self-representations reflected whatever version of American identity prevailed in her geosocial arena. Her wish was to "fit in."

I went through a period of coming to the U.S. and wanting to be accepted by Americans, not black or whites, but Americans. Becoming so Americanized, and so white because when we lived in New York, my father then moved us to Los Angeles, Pasadena, which is lily white where we lived. And I went to school with lily white kids. And I had this Valley Girl accent.

Bridget moved to the San Francisco Bay Area to attend one of its universities. She met and married an African American, and by entering the black community, her identity was transformed.

When I met my husband, I finally got to meet black Americans, which is what I wanted. So now I sound very much like a black American, but it's a conscious effort. I want to sound like a black American when I speak.

But with this identific transformation, Bridget became sensitized to the realities of American racism: "I learned racism when I met my husband, to tell you the truth, because he came from Florida and he's known it since he was a kid. It seems like a lot of his impressions are now on me."

Bridget joined a large firms in the Bay Area as an analyst and soon moved up to divisional head. But her perspective reflected that of an African American professional:

A black American, particularly if they have exposure or a degree, it's very intimidating for a lot of white Americans, so they treat you differently. They hold you back. They find ways to keep you down. I've seen that happen on jobs. And that's happened with me because they think I'm a black American. I understand the history and why things are the way they are and have found myself becoming part of that. Because I'm identified as a black American. So the thing I identify, again, with the way they treat me on the job, a black female on the job. And how far they let you go. They think about your aggressive personality, and all black American females, especially when you're up and coming on a job, that's the first thing they say about you. "You're too aggressive, or you're too assertive."

Successful African Americans are tempted to escape American discourses of difference because it is an effort to locate themselves outside American racialized definitions in order to realize their humanity. That is the reason that they assume African-centered diasporic identities. And this was the route that Bridget took. She came to the West Indian community almost by accident, through her husband. While a law student in 1990, he had heard about the San Francisco Carnaval and West Indians' participation in the event. Bridget immediately decided to become involved. After nearly twenty-five years in the United States, she used the opportunity provided by West Indian cultural organization to find her roots.

For Bridget, the West Indies represented an escape from the rigidities of American racial discourse. She speaks in almost idyllic terms of the fluidity and permeability of race relations in the Caribbean:

So you know the white people, and I was just talking to this guy, a black American guy on my job about this because he's been down to the West Indies a couple times and he loves it down there. And he was saying, "You know, in the West Indies it doesn't seem to be a problem that black and white have kids, Indian and black have kids, everybody down there is mixed." Here, it's a concern you're walking down the street with a white man, or an Asian man with a black woman. It just isn't something you see readily.

Once introduced to the West Indian community, Bridget began to embrace it wholeheartedly. She became active in West Indian organizations, holding a position as an officer in one. She also became one of the organizers in a masquerade band that participated in the annual San Francisco Carnaval festivities: "I did that because I wanted to meet people in the community because I'd lived here all these years and didn't know anybody." She organized a group of West Indian women as a bridge to her own West Indian identity: "I formed the group because I needed to feel that link. And I needed to understand the culture. And I wanted to see what women my age thought." In addition, Bridget began making annual trips to her country of origin in an effort to reconnect with her roots. Bridget embarked on this search from a self-understanding of her own deep-rooted Americanness. It was an attempt to negotiate her American identity by escaping from its strictures. But the transformation was difficult:

> When I first started going back, I really felt like an outsider. Now I've kind of learned my way around and know where I want to be and stuff. But you still kind of feel like an outsider a little bit because my lifestyle is different from theirs. And I know I'm only there for a time.

Clearly, a West Indian identity came to signify for Bridget the freedom and opportunity denied to her by American racism. The themes of freedom and communality pervade her memory of childhood and also her representations of the contemporary West Indies:

> I lived a very safe life when I was down there. My grandmother was very popular. My father was very popular. My family was very popular. It was a joyous time. There were lots of people around. All the neighbors knew each other. We went to the beach on Sundays, because you lived in the Caribbean, so those kinds of things you remember. The way my grandmother cooked on Sunday. It was different. It was a very different lifestyle than when we came to the U.S. It was different. When I came home from school in the afternoons, and I played outside, and all the neighbors knew me. That kind of thing. We lived comfortably. My grandmother was a seamstress. And she seemed to have anything she could want. New curtains in the house all the time. We all wore new clothes, clean clothes, because she could sew. We ate anything we wanted.

Bridget contrasted these memories with the isolation and restrictive lifestyle of her youth in the United States. In her country of origin she lived in a spacious "four-bedroom house" and had an abundance of everything she needed. She remembered the United States as being spartan and restrictive:

> We lived in a two-bedroom apartment, a very confined space. Home from school, we were latchkey kids. My sister, my brother, and myself. Our parents worked. They didn't come home until late. We never really got a chance to play outside except maybe on Sunday. So it was very, very different. That was a culture shock in itself.

Bridget regarded the pervasive whiteness of the United States as limiting:

> I went to Catholic schools in [my country of origin], but there were black kids around me. And funny, now I realize the textbooks had black faces

in it. And I came to the U.S. and it's a total different scene. It's white faces in the book. It's white people teaching you.

But such realization came only with immersion in an African American identity:

I didn't notice racism to say, "They treated me this way." I can't do that. Racism I learned as I got older. But actually as soon as I got out of high school, I learned racism, which is pretty late. But that's when I learned it because my father doesn't recognize it. He tries to block it out. And I guess he kept us away from it.

In Bridget's racialized conceptualizations there are clear benefits to being "foreign" as a racial minority, which partly explains the reconstitution of her identity:

In jobs, white Americans are very accepting of people who are from other countries. They treat black Americans very differently on the jobs than they do an Asian, particularly in this area. I can speak for the Asian culture, because there are so many of them here. I can also speak of Hispanics, too, because I lived in L.A.

Bridget sees in the West Indies opportunities that are foreclosed to African Americans. While she understands that West Indians are forced to come to the United States "to get an education," she sees very few benefits in immigrating, even for those seeking opportunities to earn a higher income. Clearly, the quality of life in the West Indies is much more appealing to her. And while incomes may be lower there, they buy many more of the material comforts than even a higher income can in the United States:

And it's important in the West Indies that they keep up with the Joneses, so to speak. So everybody's got two and three cars, and very little roadway. Everybody has two and three microwaves. You know, they have everything we have here. My cousins my age live as I do. Their houses are nicer than mine. Or they have more cars than we do. They make less money than I do, but the quality of life is different. Their kids are in private school. They pay for their kids.

As it turned out, Bridget was not seeking a rejection of her American identity but an accommodation between her newly discovered blackness and her recovered West Indian identity that provided an escape from its strictures. In the process, she began to distinguish between her social identity as "black" and her cultural identity as West Indian. This dualism freed her from the limitations of both. Although she identified herself as "black, just black." this referred to her social being. At the same time, she harbored deep notions of African American cultural in-effectuality, if not dysfunction:

> But so as far as values are concerned, black American culture is so despondent that you don't even know if they have any. They have one month out of the year they get to celebrate black history. They have one, what? Martin Luther King as a legal holiday. So how much value can you put to that? Black Americans, they have Kwanzaa, they celebrate at Christmas, and yes, they do the best they can. Now they're wearing African garb, and everyone's into that. It's a moneymaking thing for a lot of people. So they have their values that they're holding on to, and society will water-wash it for you so that it's not as strong as you would like it.

Bridget sees her West Indian identity as giving her the strong cultural foundation that is absent among African Americans:

> I think my culture is strong enough that I certainly make it a part of our life. I intend to keep my cultural part of my life. It's important to me when I became thirty that I identify with my culture because I don't necessarily identify strictly with black American culture because I'm not a black American. So it's real important to me that I have that heritage and I understand my culture, and I be a part.

But to Bridget, West Indian culture was important as a bridge to the wider society not available to African Americans:

> White Americans treat us very differently. White Americans tend to treat us a lot nicer than they do black Americans because we're not a black American. So we're easily accepted, treated really well, even Asians, and Asians, in my opinion, are some of the most imperialistic people I've come across. And they too tend to be more accepting of you.
>
> But the one thing I will tell you about me is I am very interested in other cultures. And one of my girlfriends pointed out, "It's because you're from another culture. So you tend to be. . . ." I'm drawn to, I have my Asian friends because they're from a different culture. And I have a couple African friends because they're from another culture. And I have, when I was in school, I had a couple friends from Iran and stuff. Again, it was a different culture, so I was attracted to that. A lot of black American kids are not exposed because of economics, so how would they know?

But in her efforts to escape the strictures of American blackness, Bridget came up against the limitations of West Indianness, especially in the patriarchy that closed off opportunities for women, and this she attributes to West Indian culture:

> I watch my friends who come here, come to Berkeley. They go to school, they get their education, and they want to stay in the country. It does bother me that they don't feel the need sometime to want to go back. I understand why they don't, though, because there's more exposure here and more money here. But even if they're there, what can they do? There's not enough jobs. Listening to their concerns about just as women, women have made some strides in the West Indies, but not as much as you would like. So they're still second-class citizens there. A lot of women in my country of origin were committing suicide. And it was going unnoticed in the newspaper. Little articles back in the back somewhere where you can't even see it. And we were trying to understand what that was from. And then I was listening to each of the women talk about what they thought it was from. And it was coming from despondence. A lot of women not being able to do the things they wanted to do.

Once Bridget's cultural roots were reestablished and replenished by annual visits to her country of origin, she began to distance herself from the West Indian community and to stop socializing with its members. She explained that the group of West Indian women that she organized "disbanded" because "people didn't have the time." She withdrew her engagement with the West Indian "lifestyle" in the San Francisco Bay Area, and she ended most of her social relationships with West Indians: "When we see each other, we greet each other and I try to support some of the things they're doing. But I also get bored with some of the stuff." She kept only a "couple of West Indian friends" because "I have other friends I hang out with."

In her most revealing decision, Bridget became an American citizen, after thirty years as a permanent resident. She filed for citizenship at the very time she was withdrawing from the West Indian social milieu. It seemed as if she had finally found a comfort zone in American society that allowed her to accept her own Americanness. In sum, participation in West Indian culture did not necessarily bring with it an identity of belonging. Bridget became resigned to the fact that she was American, as reflected in the difficulty she has had with the West Indian accent: "When I try to sound like a West Indian, I don't do a very good job, and I get teased by family who say I need to work on it. "You sound like a water wash" is what they call it. It doesn't sound authentic." Her quest was for cultural and social authenticity which she realized by drawing on different and perhaps contradictory participatory experiences. This allowed her to be American and be "black" without representing herself as "African American" as understood in popular consciousness. What emerged challenged this understanding and rejected its implications for African American cultural formation.

West Indian culture was the means that Bridget used to escape the confinement of an American identity while retaining a blackness that had a very American social construction. Only when she had resolved the dilemmas of identity could she accommodate what was fundamentally her African American social self. She tried to do this while retaining the images of freedom that seemed to define her childhood.

Bridget remained a product of the sociocultural milieu of the New York City West Indian community, with its predisposition to American forms of ethnicization and its possibilities for African Americanization. In the process, by reasserting her West Indian culture, she became an ethnicized African American in her self-representation. Her immigrant background made such a choice available to her. Otherwise, like other successful African Americans, she would have been forced to invent an African cultural origin.

John Connarly

West Indian immigrants may arrive with conceptualizations of their own blackness that may conflict with personal and collective American ideas about blackness. Manifestations of African nationalism have given a national identity—a deeply felt racial pride—to black creoles in the Caribbean, and some immigrants have brought this identific baggage with them to the United States. When it is combined with opportunities for upward mobility, it can lead to a rejection of African Americanness. The popular view of African Americans as social and cultural failures can conflict with assertions of an Africanness rooted in notions of collective historical accomplishment and cultural predispositions to achievement in the face of racial oppression. These may lead to a "dual" association. African nationalists may try to enter white society on their merits and to gain the privileges accorded to whites. Or they may seek social and intimate relations with persons of African descent. The West Indian identity accommodates the rejection of American blackness. At the same time, the African nationalists among them may want to associate with persons in the black community who exhibit the requisite qualities of African pride. They may also refuse to associate with West Indians on similar grounds.

John Connarly immigrated to the United States in 1974 when he was twenty years old. This was a period of heightened Afro-Caribbean na-tionalist sentiment, particularly among the youth and members of the region's upwardly mobile upper tier of the black lower classes and the lower middle classes. He describes his background as "more or less above poverty, I guess bordering around middle class. In other words, we were pretty—we were comfortable. There were times when things were very rough and very tough, but there wasn't a lot of money float-ing around." His father was a fisherman who turned his trade into a small business. John came to the United States on a student visa and enrolled in a college in the South. He graduated with a science degree.

John came to the United States with an Africa-centered philosophy that included identific conceptualizations of self. He describes himself as an African West Indian, an identity that assumes an association with per-sons of African descent. His expectations on arriving in the United States were that "I would come and be around another set of African people from the diaspora, and perhaps we can work together—from the impres-sions I had back in home living around mostly Africans, I thought that it would probably be the same when I came to the United States."

Even though John's pattern of social affinities remained consistently and exclusively "African centered," he quickly began to distinguish be-tween his own brand of blackness and African Americanness: "After arriving here, I realized that there's a lot of animosity between African Americans and those Africans coming from outside of America from the West Indies or from Africa." This he attributed to a crisis of iden-tity among African Americans because of their separation from their African roots:

[African Americans] are a lost tribe. They have no clear-cut identity as to who they are. And I find that they ultimately seek to assimilate. In other words, like my mother puts it sometimes, hanging your mouth where the soup is falling. Wherever it's falling, that's where you're going to hang your mouth, as opposed to standing on one's own, you know, one's own feet, and establishing one's self. There's always this grappling of hands, hands stretching out looking for someone to assist versus finding ways to assist one's own self. And I make it as a generalized statement because even though you have individuals who have managed to move beyond a certain level, once they have moved, they tend to forget and seek to become more associated with another race of people, another class of people, and eventually do not necessarily identify themselves as being, as being Africans. I had a conversation—I've had several conversations with people who have told me that, you know, they have long since dropped the word *African* from their name. They are black, and black's not a race. See, there's no clear, clean indication that you are identifying with a particular race as far as African Americans, I find, in this country are concerned.

In John's understanding of African Americans, this absence of identity leads to divisiveness and the absence of social cohesion:

It nonetheless keeps things so divisive and so separated, and you're not able to really come together on any one common ground, and it makes it difficult to approach situations and to deal with problems. Everyone has, rightfully so, their own views and their own opinions as to how things can be solved.

John sees this crisis of identity as the distinguishing feature between "Africans from the outside" and African Americans, and he believes that the distinction is evident in the former's predisposition to accomplishment. This is recognized even by whites. While John does not attribute his own success to his West Indian identity, his West Indianness nonetheless becomes the signifying element:

I think that even before, looking at education and looking at economic standards, white Americans look straight at the color initially. And after you open your mouth and you begin to speak, they detect a difference between your mode of speech versus that of an African American, and immediately it tends to—something tends to change in the way that they interface and interact. Exactly what that's about, I can only offer my own opinions and perspectives on what I feel, what I think it is because once they begin to ask you, "Where are you from? You have an accent?" it sets up another stage of communication. From my own personal experience, I noticed that based on the manner in which I conduct myself in conversations, in addressing people, it tended to perhaps ease a strain of tensions that normally would exist between blacks and white with this veil of racism existing. And they—I don't know— perhaps felt that they were dealing with a person that was much better educated and therefore had to deal with them on a different level. I think the basic impression of whites toward Africans in this country is that, one, they do not have that foundation in terms of their education, and they tend to abuse that.

Paradoxically, John believes that African Americans' failure is partly self-imposed by their attitude toward success. He believes that Africans from the "outside" understand this perfectly and that this has served them well in their efforts to negotiate American success:

> It took years and years of experience, being confronted with certain kinds of remarks and so on, to realize that in my view, one, there was fear on the part of the African Americans that someone who has come from the outside can come and do so much better than they have been able to do, and two, the manner in which other people, other races, treated Africans from outside of the United States was quite different from the way in which African Americans were being treated.

To John, the problem for African Americans is their failure to understand and intellectually engage the society in which they live. That is, they could use rationality to overcome the problem of racial oppression.

> I think one of the limitations that I have noticed is that people tend to hold on to this notion of racism and for the most part, I don't think they really understand the nature of racism. It's an emotional reaction, and an emotional response, and I think it takes a little bit more than emotions to deal with the whole body of racism because in itself I feel it's an organization just like any other organization. It's an "ism" like communism, socialism, racism. It's a structure. It's something that was put together, and there's a reason for it being put together in that manner. I think for the most part here in the United States, African Americans do not look at the broader picture of racism. They look only at prejudices, and they sometimes even when confronted with prejudices, call it racism when it's not true. But racism by definition is a belief, a system of beliefs that one people or race holds of being superior over another people. So the whole thing is about superiority, inferiority. And hence we get all the notions of white supremacy and the like, and I think if it were to be looked at from that standpoint, one would begin to understand what kind of factors go into creating a structure as such to establish that superiority that one feels one needs to have.

It is clear that, to John, the reality of America blinds African Americans to the truth of their own condition. Coming from "outside," however, overcomes this limitation:

> Coming from another place, country, another culture, being around other people, exposed to other things sort of helped me to look at the much broader picture of situations versus you know, approaching things from a limited view.

John sees members of the West Indian community to be at risk from the American practices and understandings that have been so detrimental to African Americans. He sees this in their desire for material possessions, which can trap West Indians in the discourse that is at the core of American capitalism:

> I see Caribbean people pretty much isolated, not necessarily from each other, but only in terms of where they have chosen to live, and the things they have decided that they would do to progress and to move forward and so on, and also perhaps of the intensity of what they have chosen to do, which is maybe working two jobs, three jobs, become very preoccupied with that, and you know, have not necessarily been able to get together. From my perspective, we have lost some ties, or we have not sought to continue to maintain or to reestablish the kinds of ties which we did have back in the Caribbean. The close connection, the family working together, the extended family, and so on and so forth. But I think that if there are groups of people, friends, and so on, if called upon for certain things, I think that they would respond to a certain extent depending on the level of the friendship. But other than that, they're still somewhat separate, one from the other. I can even go as far as to say you know, there is a semblance of assimilation into American society, American culture, beginning to take on the mentalities of African Americans here, whether it is to establish a difference of one toward the other, or just simply as a result of once again, the things which they are pursuing and want to focus more on those things.

For John, then, the West Indian community does not offer the solidarity and ties that he can use to negotiate a location in American society. This has prompted him to form individual relationships with members of the middle-class African American community who share his Africa-centered ideology. All of John's affective relationships have been with middle-class African American women who share his philosophy of African pride and African collective and individual achievement. Two of these relationships produced children, and he was married to an African American woman at the time of the interview.

At the same time, John's entrance into American society is almost stereotypically that of the permanent foreigner who embarks on a path of political invisibility and social innocuousness. The reason had to do with what he perceived as his rejection by the African American community: "I'm still considered as being a foreigner to a lot of black people, and so long as that feeling and notion is there, I'm always a stranger to them. I don't feel accepted by Americans here." As a "foreigner," John is particularly sensitive to the consequences of political assertiveness. He thus decided to keep his views to himself because he does not want to risk being a "target":

> I am just a person who likes to voice my opinions about things, and I want to be very—to be able to voice my opinions without running into any serious conflicts that may result in one taking the, you know—the advantage of that to dispense of, of an individual. I think that part of the political structure here is one in which it is very protective, and it's very wary of people who try to point out its faults and so on.

At the same time, John believes that "we have to be instrumental in finding ways in which to assist people with problems." He concentrated on the problems of the African American community and started a professional career of service to that community by joining a public agency dealing with inner-city youth. He quickly moved up to be the head of one of the agency's branches.

John has managed to retain the black identity that he rescued from the baggage of his social location in Caribbean society. At the same time, he has developed and maintains a cognitive distinction between himself and "African Americans." He recognizes the crisis of racism but sees in his own personal life and philosophy the means to defy it. This has led to a view of African Americans similar to that in the white imagination. From his perspective, African Americans can overcome the artificiality of racism by adopting his philosophy of African solidarity and African pride. The responsibility is theirs to end racism's deleterious effects. But their deep-rooted Americanness has prevented their salvation.

John sees his own life as an example of the possibilities of liberation. His life was forged from his diasporic origins outside the American— and particularly the black American—social construction. His retention of his West Indian identity supports his own self-representation as a permanent foreigner. His philosophy has propelled him to missionary-like work in the African American community. In this way, he is able to retain and justify his "African" identity while, at the same time, sustaining cognitive distinctions of difference between himself and African Americans. His foreignness legitimizes the absence of personal political engagement even while his African consciousness dictates his social engagement with the black community. In the process, John has managed to bridge the contradictions between his self-identity, on the one hand, and American conceptualizations of blackness, on the other, in ways that maintain the integrity of his African-centered consciousness. He regards himself as the social and cultural superior of African Americans, a superiority that is tied to the particularities of his West Indian origin.

Jayne Jonas

Social and cultural alienation and economic marginalization may cause immigrants to reject identific self-representation with their community of origin and to seek from other groups alternative forms of belonging. But their efforts may be hampered by discourses of difference in their host society that can limit the possibilities of constructing an identity. Although an African American identity is available to West Indian immigrants in the United States, experiences of alienation and rejection may foreclose this choice. Those whose identities are not grounded in their community of origin may find themselves in a perpetual state of anomie. They can be dragged down in a perpetual quest for belonging, even seeking out opportunities that are precluded by the host society's sociocultural discourse of difference.

Immigrating at a young age can prove socially and culturally dislocating, especially when one is isolated from one's community of origin. When an immigrant's culture is reinforced by the representations and practices of a nuclear or extended family, the possibilities for social and cultural acceptance by segments of the host community also may be limited. The immigrant may then be left in a sociocultural limbo, unable to negotiate a way into the host society and unable to discard the symbolic cues of belonging associated with the community of origin.

Jayne Jones immigrated from the West Indies to the United States in 1974 when she was thirteen years old. She came after years of separation from her mother who had immigrated much earlier and left her in the care of other family members. Her recollections of her country of origin are of intense poverty, physical abuse, and shame, accompanied by a deep sense of separation from her mother who, even while in the United States, continued to be the main provider and to maintain strong maternal bonds with her several children who were left behind. Her recollections of life in her homeland are interspersed with tragedies of death. She recalls the death of "fourteen of her grandmother's kids," the death of her best friend by accident, and the death of her siblings. Her only happy memories of home were of her relationship with her mother:

> I don't have any good memories [of home], except being there with [my] mom. My mom would bring things for us. She would stay home and take care of her kids. My dad was a bad man, really, really bad. So I grew up—I actually was in a very abusive home. The only person, the only love that I think I ever really felt was for my mom, because she was always there.

When Jayne's mother left for the United States, it was quite traumatic and socially disruptive and left Jayne without a means of developing a sense of social security. Her mother's leaving also led to separation from her siblings. Nonetheless, Jayne explained her mother's departure in altruistic terms:

> When she got the opportunity to come to America, because she wanted a better life for her kids, she took it. We stayed with my sister. But my sister was a road runner. So we did all the work and whatever, but she was a good sister, also. She was the eldest. Then, when she left, we went to live with our grandmother. Then with my mom's sister—it was all of them were living in a house.
>
> Like I said, there was no really, no good times in between there. When you think you were so happy, you look back. We were separated—what my mom's family did—or my grandmother—they took the two girls, my sister and I, they kept us, but they left my three brothers in the house where we used to live, where we grew up in. So, and we wouldn't see each other.

The result, for Jayne, was a rejection of her cultural background and an inclination not to return to her homeland:

> Like I said, there's the good, the bad, and the ugly. We had our shares of the ugly part. Before my mom left, it was tough, but still, don't matter what, once your mom is around, you have that security. You have that security, but once you've gone, your whole world seems like it's shattered and most of that . . . nope, I won't go back right now.

She embraced the chance to immigrate to the United States and created in her mind heavenly images of America:

Before I came, I always had this impression that America was such a green place. You always think, "Oh, you're going to have all the apples you can eat. Cheese. Everything. Grapes. You never saw what a grape was like until [my mother] started sending them back. So you would think, "Oh, America's going to be one of these places that's going to be oh, so fabulous. All the houses are really white."

Jayne's mother's decision, in 1974, to sponsor all her children to come to the United States represented, to Jayne, the solution to her family's social dislocation. She spoke excitedly about this reunification:

[My mother] got her visa and she came out here. Then she decided to come back, she went back to get us. She filed the papers and it was so funny. At the time, they were giving out green cards at the airport. So we came to America and then we stood up in a line. We came to America and we got a green card at the airport. It was stamped at the airport. The only thing that we got in the mail was a Social Security card. We never went down to Social Security office—nothing. Everything was given to us. Within a week, we had the Social Security card, the same day in 1974—it was stamped right there. The green card didn't ever expire. So that's why we came.

Immigration did not end the family's poverty. Her mother had a job in the low-paying care services as a personal helper to an infant, and Jayne's family lived in the Bedford-Stuyvesant district of Brooklyn, one of New York City's most economically depressed areas. This was where Jayne spent her adolescent years and where she was introduced to African Americans. The experience proved to be quite alienating:

When we looked across the street, there we saw a bar. All these junkies. I didn't know what drugs or what . . . we were so—man, we were so naive. We lived in the heart of Bedford-Stuyvesant. That was a part of Brooklyn, at the time, that all it had was junkies. Junkies on every corner. All the junkies. There was a bar there and the music was going all night. All night. All the kids in the neighborhood did was the big MF and the F— ooooh. I had never heard a kid curse. We were so scared of America, to cross the street where all these junkies and stuff . . . my mother prayed and prayed and prayed.

These first impressions shaped Jayne's attitude toward African Americans, for whom she developed a deep disdain. She attributes her attitude to their rejection of West Indians. Despite enrolling in a high school that was "95 percent white," Jayne believes that African Americans made her school experience intolerable:

> I hated it. You know why? Black Americans do not like people from the Caribbean. They don't . . . me and my brother, we were going to school. We started school. We had to take three trains over to the school because our school was in Queens. The kids would stand on the steps when you down on the subway, and they wouldn't let us pass. Yeah, the black Americans were the ones that never liked us. They were so naive that everybody—African, or they had some kind of African background, whatever—they never believed that. So they would tell us things like, "Go back to where you came from." Because of our accent—oooh, they hated it. We can't pronounce the words, how they say it or whatever, they use a lot of slangs that we didn't know about. So they would tease us. Oh, they would tease us. It was awful. I got into so many fights. In those days it was all African Americans. They were part—like I said, they would make fun of us and tell us to go back on the ship, to go back to where we came from. I kicked a couple of them down escalators.

African Americans also had a profoundly negative effect on her brother:

> They used to—my brother was shorter than me. I don't know how come everybody passed me now, but—and they would bother him. He wouldn't talk. My brother is still very quiet. He's married and got a child, but he's still quiet. He was extremely quiet. These black Americans, oh, man, they treated us like dirt.

Jayne developed a particularly condemnatory understanding of African Americans:

> I think they're getting—I think instead of New York getting—instead of them now improving, it's getting worse. Because these people out here, they keep holding on and holding on—"Well, he did this to me and America did this to me." America didn't do nothing to you. You had it all. You just don't want to take it. Like I always believed, if there ever becomes a black president, this country's doomed. It's doomed. I don't care what they tell me because they do not want to get up and go. They want the easiest way out. They don't want to work for anything. It's like it has to be given. . . . It has to be given to them.

She also became oblivious to the issues that were of concern to African Americans:

Even when they started the—what do you call it—busing in school fighting, the black against the white and black—we never joined in because we didn't know what it was what they were fighting for. The only person—as a matter of fact, they switched my hours of time to go to school because they were bothering me so much, pick fights with me, that I would fight with them. I started breaking umbrellas on any one of them that messed with me.

Jayne's rejection of African Americans was accompanied by a positive attitude toward the material benefits of America, and she remembers the material circumstances of her life in Brooklyn:

We went to an apartment—my mom had a two-bedroom apartment. Inside, my sister—because she loved to decorate at the time—she was helping my mom because she came in 1971. They had—as a matter of fact—I have never seen red carpets. Red carpets on the floor. My sister had her living room—there were mirrors on the walls, diamond shaped—really, the house was in red and gold. The apartment building was nice. It was a nice brownstone. There were three floors. We lived on the first floor. We had never seen, like I said, carpeted floor. We had never seen, because everything back home was hardwood floor. Everything—the refrigerator, the nice drapes—just how you see in the magazines, there goes—my mom's apartment, my sister's and mom's apartment, was like that.

While attending a predominantly white high school, Jayne developed a special affinity with white Americans. They became a refuge from the inhospitable African American world.

We wanted to be OK, but it was hard. Everything—we toughed it out. It was rough on my mom. It was really, really hard. Then we ended up, my mom—and then the system, you had to register the children at the Unified School District. Oh, man, I'll tell you. It was hard. Then, at first at school, I cried. I wanted to go home. We took—the school that we ended up going to when we started in September, it was an hour and a half away because by the time we came to be registered to go to the school in the area, they were already full. So we had to take three trains to get to that school. We were like "OK." We ended up in a school that was predominately white. We all went to Richmond Hill High in Queens. Ninety-five percent of it was white. All white. That's why I talk like this and get along so good with the whites. So, that's what we did.

Jayne also seemed to be entertaining the possibility of becoming part of the white community:

It seems like I wasn't so much around the black people. I didn't really hang out with too much black Americans. I was in college and high school with the white people. It's so funny. I went to high school. Ninety-five percent of it was white, I told you. Then when I left there, I went to a business school. I was the only black girl. The business school was all white.

This set the stage for her sense of social alienation. The discourse of difference precluded a white identity, despite her affinity with whites. Her sense of rejection by African Americans prevented her from identifying with their community. But Jayne's desire to establish social and cultural links with the West Indian community were weak, at best. She considered the West Indian community in New York to be "segregated" and constraining. Its members just "don't want to open up":

The Caribbean people back then, in New York, they weren't together. They're not a together community. Like if you were in a Trinidadian house, a Trinidadian party—it's a Trinidadian party. You go to a Jamaican party. You go to a Guyanese party.

Jayne longed for a world free of divisions and racial boundaries, where "everybody is one. It doesn't matter, if you cut us, we're all going to bleed. It's all red. I would like to see somebody bleed some green blood somewhere—or some black one."

She dealt with her social and cultural isolation by maintaining a strong bond with her mother. She became emotionally dependent on her male partners, at least one of whom existed on the margins of society. When she was seventeen, Jayne started an affair with a twenty-seven-year-old friend of her brother's. Then she left him for another man with whom she had a child out of wedlock. At the time, she was twenty and was forced, because of the pregnancy, to depend on her mother. The child's father was a drug user and dealer and was murdered:

He was a good guy, but he got caught up with the wrong people. Fast money. What did I say? He got started selling drugs. I kicked him out. After my child was born, he and I lived together for like six months and I kicked him out. Actually, he was smoking the weed in the morning, noon, night. He was so hooked on marijuana and I told him, I said, "I'm going to tell you this, your body system is going to get immune to that and you'll want something stronger." "No, no." Yes, it did. I kicked him out. The first thing I started smelling was the cocaine. Kicked him out. Got to go. I went through hell. That's when you pick the wrong man, if you're looking for love, you're looking in the wrong places. But he wanted fast money. They killed him. They murdered him for $10. They broke his neck. Threw him down from the sixth floor and broke his neck.

Jayne continued her relationship with him until he died, and their relationship grew even stronger after her mother died in 1983. Jayne went on welfare while studying for an associate degree in a technical field. After her child's father was killed, she resumed her relationship with her earlier lover, who also abused drugs. She lost her job and, with it, the ability to support herself.

It was at this point that she decided to move to California, at the urging of some of her siblings who already were there. She was pregnant when she moved. When she arrived, Jayne became acutely aware of her position on the social and economic margins of California's West Indian community, and this affected her relationship with her California family: "I'm the only one that's not married in the family. I'm the only one whose been through hell and back."

Jayne's siblings had, in one way or another, become part of the ethos of West Indian accomplishment in Northern California, but it was evident that Jayne did not fit the West Indian profile of achievement and stability. Her relationship with her siblings broke down. She recalls that she "went through hell with my family." As a result, she was forced to live in a motel that catered to the homeless, which is where her second child was born. At that point, she "decided it was time to get a grip. I decided I'm going to put respect back into my life—with a family around or nobody." She began making an effort at socioeconomic respectability. She found a temporary job just to make ends meet and eventually secured a full-time job at a major utility company in Northern California. Although she married the father of her second child, the marriage did not last because he did not fit the self-understandings of West Indians in the San Francisco Bay that were driving Jayne's ambitions. She "got an annulment, because he wanted to drink and use drugs, also. Kicked him out. I said enough is enough."

Based on her experiences in early childhood, Jayne had learned to respond to her social and economic deprivation and marginalization with withdrawal and disparagement, a response that continued after her move to California. Although she tried to "blend in" with the social and cultural mores of the West Indian community in California, she was unsuccessful. So she began to disparage its sense of social and economic superiority:

Sometimes they just tick me off. I think they're very selfish. I don't know what it is that's wrong with them. I don't know. I always feel we all went through the same thing, in a way. Yours might be a little deeper than mine or whatever, but everybody came to American to improve themselves. Nobody is going to leave a rich country and come up here. All of us have to be some way or another in—in kind of a remote situation. Nobody's a millionaire out here.

She further suggested that all West Indians are the "same," no matter what their social origin or economic position back home: "Once you come to this country and you're here, don't come here and say you expect to be treated like royalty." Indeed, she began equating the West Indian community with the African American community, which she continued to despise. Now, however, she saw the West Indians as the contaminating influence, since they were the ones who violated [white] American notions of equality. She believes that the lesson of America is that "everybody is one" and that West Indians need to learn this. So she decried the tendency for Americans to mimic West Indian tastes, styles, and attitudes:

If you notice now, finally, if you notice—if you talk to an African American person, a lot of times they try to speak with an accent. The way they dress—with the dreadlocks, the hair. . . . The way how they dress is not—they're trying to be more Caribbean or West Indian than anything else.

At the same time, Jayne accused the West Indian community of the same type of prejudice toward African Americans that she experienced with them in New York. She reprimanded the West Indians for not liking African Americans:

Now they're the ones now turned around and don't like them because of the way they come up and try to do the things that we do. Like, in the carnivals, the weekend, our carnivals is basically—it's more Americans than Caribbean people. They'll go, "Oh, you think you're West Indian . . ." and they go off. But to me, this—there's so much to share and learn from each other. There's no way that anybody should get all jealous and get mad. I don't know why. But see—I guess, to each his own. To each his own. It's how you feel.

And at this point, Jayne claims common cause with the African American community, seeing herself as a victim of the identical type of prejudice that West Indians exhibit toward African Americans:

To me, I have a lot of support from—now—in my adult age, with African Americans. I don't have support from my own Caribbean people because they know you from when—the way that you were raised back then or whatever; a little bit about you or your culture or whatever, they kind of treat you like they expect you to stay there. It's like, no.

But nonetheless her disparagement of the African American community has continued. Her attitude toward other racialized and immigrant communities was determined by their perceived relationship with African Americans:

The Chicanos and the Mexicans, basically, they're just basically trying to be American, period. They want to fit in so badly, with them, with black Americans, that they believe black Americans is it. They try to speak like them. You hear the slangs. They're kind of on the same level. Yeah. They kind of get into—well, now, they really kind of get together. I'm looking at the way they dress and everybody. I don't know. Why do you guys have to copy? Why can't you do your own thing? It's like, I look at them and I'm thinking, "Gee, if everybody would just be your own self. You don't have to do—I know most of you Mexicans and stuff, they don't want to be raised like that. But they want to fit in so badly. They want—it's Puerto Rico or Mexican—one of them keep saying, "Our state is an American state." I don't even know which . . . I don't even know, but they just feel that they have to fit in. So they try . . . and then they get the thing that the white people treat them . . . and that is not true. I don't think.

At the same time, Jayne sees California as offering the possibility of cross-racial and cross-cultural relations. This was the first thing that caught her eye almost as soon as she landed in the state, and it was a refreshing change from the "segregation" of New York:

When I walked into the club—I went, "Oh, here's a Nigerian and he's with a white girl," I was stunned. I walked in that night because I came in with eleven pieces of luggage in 1987. It was everybody was one. That's why when—my girlfriends come here, they come to visit—they go, "Damn, you guys are all mixed up." That's the only way you learn.

It nonetheless is evident that Jayne does not want to be "one" with African Americans or any group associated with them. At the same time, she is clearly a social isolate in the West Indian community. Her response was one of near self-abnegation. She turned next to the Asian community, mainly to Filipinos. Curiously, she sees in this group the

qualities that define West Indianness. She also considers Filipinos willing to accept West Indians and to reject African Americans. Indeed,
their attractiveness seems to be what she describes as a perpetual state
of conflict with the latter:

> When I look at it now, I look at American being, African American and the
> Asians, they are fighting and they are bickering, but if somebody from our
> culture, the people from the Caribbean, the Asian community accepts us
> more than the black African American. I think they consider themselves a
> minority in their own way, too. You know what I mean? From a different
> . . . in a way, they have similar customs to us. I think they consider them-
> selves a minority in their own way, too. You know what I mean? From a
> different . . . in a way, they have similar customs to us.

Jayne's best friend is a Filipina, a relationship seems to have developed, from her perspective, into one that resembles a family. She describes her as a "sister":

> My best friend, she's Filipino, her daughter calls me Aunty Jayne. She
> tells everybody, "I have a sister. You've got to see my sister." So when I
> went to their events, her people say: "I didn't know your sister was
> black." "Yeah!" Because we are so close. She's the only daughter for her
> mom, but it's like we're in the same bed. We do everything together.
> We're just one. That is really, really good.

Despite her social marginalization from the West Indian community
and her cultural self-abnegation, Jayne's self-understandings have produced a pattern of association typical of the West Indian community in
California. She will not identify with African Americans and subscribes
to many of the popular negative stereotypes of them. She sees herself as
West Indian in terms that suggest equality with whites, and she distinguishes herself from African Americans by her foreignness. In turn, in
her foreignness, she sees social and cultural similarities with the Asian
community. These explain the affinities between Asians and West Indians and their shared hostility to African Americans. Jayne regards as
anathema any attempt at accepting African American cultural and social forms. This, in her mind, condemns the Mexican and Latino populations. She thinks that Latinos have rejected their unique foreignness
and have become like African Americans. As a result, they have sunk to
"the same level." Jayne thus sees herself as a permanent foreigner with
no desire to return to her country of origin, which, she believes, would
be "dangerous" to the health of her daughter. She explained that in

order to survive her country of origin, her daughter would "have to wait until she's sixty years old, when her immune system really builds up." This provides a legitimate reason for remaining in the United States while refusing to identify with it, because, for her, to be American is to be African American. At the same time, Jayne admits some affinity with African Americans in the face of prejudice, even when it is the prejudice of the West Indian community.

Jessica Barker

Class dynamics, participatory experiences, and the social culture of location of residence are the determining factors in the construction of an identity. These can combine to reinforce a West Indian identity even under conditions of American ethnicization or African Americanization.

West Indians' relations with African Americans are ambiguous, as reflected in West Indians' representations and cognitive constructs of African Americans. At the same time, West Indians must deal with the reality of American racism. On the one hand, they use their West Indian identity and their status as a permanent foreigner as a way of separating from the American racial discourse. On the other, as blacks, West Indians must continually deal with the consequences of racism and its implications for everyday interaction. The greater the exposure to American racism, the more sympathetic and benign are West Indians' understandings of African Americans.

Jessica Barker arrived in the United States when she was only seven years old, and so she has only a superficial memory of life in her country of origin. Her memories of her West Indian childhood are a combination of West Indian concepts of difference and American exoticized images of the West Indies.

Jessica's memories of her childhood have affected her understanding of her West Indian difference. Jessica sees her West Indian identity as reinforced by African American prejudice against West Indians. At the same time, she sees the basis for an identity shared by West Indians and African Americans. The problem is that this commonality is not recognized by the African American community:

> Growing up in New York City, there was a lot of prejudice against West Indians at that time, in the 1960s, early 1970s. There was a lot of prejudice when I was attending school. I went to Catholic school in New

York. Prejudice from other black people, black American people. They would call us West Indian monkeys. Get back on your banana boat. It kind of surprised me, because there's enough prejudice from other cultures, and then when your own people are turning around and doing this to you, it's kind of funny. It was very hurtful, because I wanted to become friends with these people, and they did not want to become friends with me. So, every day, there was some kind of fight. I would come home crying, because I was in a fight, because of being from the Caribbean.

At the same time, experiences of racial discrimination and racial prejudice during numerous visits to the American South became deeply ingrained in Jessica's psyche and produced a sympathetic understanding of, if not sense of affinity with, African Americans. She became extremely sensitive to racial insults:

We used to spend our summers in the South, and there were still black and white bathrooms. So that is a specific example, you know, [in] 1968, 1969, there were still black and white bathrooms. I got on a plane a couple of years ago, and they called first-class passengers, and I boarded the plane and the white flight attendant came over to me and wanted to know, where was my seat? And I said, "I'm sitting right there." And then after that, I went back over to him and I wanted to know why he asked me where I was sitting, because they always ask first-class passengers to board first. So that was another example. I'll be in a store shopping and maybe buying an expensive item, and a white person might not take care of me or will say, "Do you know how much that costs?" You know, thinking that I can't afford it. A lot of people ask me, what my husband, well, I've been asked by white people, many times, when I tell them my husband works for an airline company, the first thing that come out of their mouth, they want to know if he is a baggage handler? I don't work, they want to know, they assume that I'm on welfare, when I'm not. I pay for school. So, to this day questions are being asked. Are you on welfare and this is being asked by white people.

Before moving in 1988 to California, Jessica spent fifteen years in New York City. She was less specific about the development of her sense of identity during the years she spent in the city. It appears, however, that she became an ethnicized West Indian American. She indicates that her relationships with African Americans improved significantly, and she attributes this to the greater presence of West Indians: "Later on in life I really didn't have a problem, because I guess in New York City, compared to California, you have such an influx of West Indian people from the different Caribbean islands, that later on in life, West Indian people began to be accepted." What is clear, however, is that Jessica became very Americanized over the years, to the point that West Indians failed to recognize her background. She attributes this to her immigrating during childhood: "From growing up here, most West Indian people would say that I'm an American, because I have been here since I was seven."

Jessica met a West Indian in New York who was about to be transferred by his company. She moved with him to Northern California to get married and set up a household. When she arrived, she had clerical experience and had paraprofessional training. At first she worked in a paraprofessional field and then enrolled in a community college. Later she transferred to one of Northern California's universities and eventually earned a degree in a technical discipline. At the time of the interview she was a full-time student. The choice of higher education was a consequence of Jessica's choice to become re–West Indianized and was undoubtedly conditioned by the mores of the West Indian community in Northern California and her husband's socioeconomic position. Because of her husband, Jessica had come to California with privileged access to the West Indian community and also the expectation that she must "live up" to the West Indians' self-image of success.

Jessica's reaccommodation to her West Indian roots was almost total: "I consider myself mostly a West Indian, because I eat the food and I play the music. My culture is very strong." In the interview, she described herself as "West Indian" despite growing up in the United States. She began visiting her country of origin at least twice a year, and she talked about plans to move back to the West Indies with her husband "in another fifteen years." And she either developed or revived her accent to the point that Americans would inquire about it: "If someone detects an accent from me, the first thing that they ask me, 'Are you from [the West Indies]?'" Her circle of friends were almost exclusively West Indian. She claims that "it just turned out that way" despite what she lamented as the dispersal of the West Indian community throughout the San Francisco Bay Area. Jessica believes that she has "common ground" with her West Indian friends in a way that she does not with Americans: "The music. Calypso, reggae, our foods, that's our common ground. Our foods like curry, curry is like a main dish in the Caribbean, and in terms of things like oxtails and eating souse and let's see, salt fish, there are so many different foods that we eat out here that

American people can not, tend not to eat." So Jessica began to make a special effort to seek out West Indians, "just meeting them through work, through school, and I just hear someone's accent and start to talk to them."

At the same time, however, Jessica's sensitivity to American racial prejudice produced a much more sympathetic understanding of African Americans than that of most people in Northern California's West Indian community. She sees herself almost as an interpreter to other West Indians of the reality of racism and the struggle of the African American community against its debilitating consequences. She explained West Indian opportunity in terms of this struggle:

> I really don't have a general impression about African Americans. Nothing bad to say, really, because I've had to kind of get on a few of my West Indian friends, or family from the Caribbean, because they will say that they don't like African Americans, and so forth. And I'm like, "You can't say that, because," and I usually go back into the history and say, "Because of the Civil Rights movement, by African Americans, black people from the different countries, whether it be Africa, wherever they are coming from, were allowed here to come and work in the United States and have equal opportunities that were provided by African American students of the rights movement." So, I usually try to make them understand that they should accept African American people.

Clearly, for Jessica, the West Indies represents the social location of racial harmony. This is one of the main distinctions that she emphasizes in her almost idyllic memories of her region of origin. She decries American ignorance of the normalcy of diversity and racial tolerance that she describes as the prevailing condition in the West Indies:

> Usually the Asian or the Latino community, they always wanted to know if there were other Asians or other Latinos living in the West Indies, because for some reason, they think that only black people live in the Caribbean. So, on perchance a white West Indian or an Asian West Indian would talk to me, they were kind of surprised to hear this accent coming from them, because they thought that only black people live in the Caribbean. I was asked that plenty of times. Yeah. I was in a bank talking to a Chinese, but he lived in Jamaica, so when he would come into the bank, he would talk to me. His name was Winston, and he would talk to me. And he had this serious Jamaican accent. And I remember one of the Asian coworkers, in fact, she was from Burma, she would come over and she would say, "Jessica, where is he from? His ac-

cent is different to Asian people?" And I told her that he was from Jamaica and she was really shocked. She said, because she thought that only black people lived there. And there was another white lady who would come in, in this bank, and would only deal with me also, and she was from my country, and so there was, like, the white people would come over and say, "Where is she from?" And I'd say, "She's from my country." And they would think, [do] white people live there? And I'm like, "Yeah."

Jessica's understanding of the Caribbean is nonetheless conditioned by a fundamental racial understanding of the United States. On the one hand, she believes that white Americans are much better informed about the West Indies and West Indians because of their exposure: "I think because, maybe, white Americans got to travel a little bit more. They more accepted West Indian people than black Americans did." However, she believes that whites' tolerance and understanding does not extend to race. Whites, she seems to suggest, are unable to accommodate racial equality. So Jessica believes that racial harmony in the West Indies is related to the social, cultural, and political dominance of blacks:

> In the Caribbean, white people, I would say white people and black people, basically, get along very well, more so, I would say the reason why is because blacks dominate the Caribbean. They are the prime ministers. They are the presidents. They are the leaders of the country. We're in charge of everything down there, so that's the difference where as up here, it's the other way around.

Jessica's understanding of the West Indies is based on the American popular imagination and the West Indian idealization of notions of origin. The West Indies is a mixture of tourist paradise and the location of true freedom and privilege acquired from the right of belonging. It is a place to be "special" and acknowledged:

> The house where we lived was in a country area and we had the beach. There is a really nice beach where you can view from the backyard of the house, and that's something that you don't really have here, too much. There were a lot of families around, aunts, uncles at all time. So, I am considered in that area where we live in my country, I am considered to be a change-of-life baby, so I grew up to be a spoiled little girl, as everyone said, because I had two big brothers to take care of me.
>
> Here you are a little bit more stressed out. In the Caribbean, people are laid back. For instance, a lot of them, when they leave work in the evenings, they have their bathing suits and they go to the beach and just

swim a little bit. As they call it, a sea bath. And then come home and do whatever they have to do. Cooking, like, for instance, on [Sunday,] eating times are different. On Sundays, in the Caribbean, you tend to eat early. You tend to eat at twelve where as here, five, six o'clock in the evening, you are now eating. You are a little bit more active, so I know, for instance, people are not really overweight or anything, because they are outdoors a whole lot more compared to here where the lifestyle is a little bit more sedentary. You still have the extended family. I know the people who I stayed with the seven years before immigration are still there. They are still there. All my aunts, my uncles, my cousins are still living with their parents, and it's OK, where as here, you go out early in life, eighteen years old, you are looking to get out on your own. They are not that way.

Similarly, Jessica's representations of West Indians are quite stereotypical. In addition to being defined by a culture of food and music, she describes West Indians as driven by a work ethic. The themes of hard work and multiple occupations have become universalized and popularized in American images of West Indian immigrants: "A lot of people come to, say, for example, New York City, because they can work two or three jobs, make a ton of money, then build their house in the Caribbean, and eventually go back there to live. And that's why they come."

Jessica's self-representation as West Indian is rooted in American stereotypical understanding. It is not so much the West Indian in her looking for a return to her country of origin, but the American in her that is seeking racial harmony and a sense of belonging. In this, she is constantly disappointed, so the West Indies has become a backdrop against which she judges the limitations of America:

And then in the summer, we used to go down South a lot, so we would drive down there, and I would wake up the next morning thinking that I was in my home country, because in the South, since it's country and the houses are not close together like you have in Brooklyn and so forth. I always would wake up the next morning and think that we were in my country. We had magically got there some kind of way, because of the country area that I was used to living in.

For Jessica, the West Indies is an escape from the racial trials of the United States in the same way that for many African Americans, Africa is an escape. But Jessica has much more direct and immediate claims of belonging and of diasporic origin outside the sociocultural geography of the United States than do African Americans. She sees in her West

Indian identity a means of negotiating a sociocultural location outside the racialized space of American difference. The West Indian community offers her an alternative "common ground" to American racial reality. But it is her participatory experiences as a black woman in America that have shaped her self-representations. So despite claims to a West Indian identity, Jessica has developed close bonds to her host country: "Since I grew up here, I love the United States, especially New York City." Her defense of African Americans in the face of West Indian intolerance is a defense of herself.

Edwin McIntosh

Through its involvement in African American institutional and associational networks, the West Indian professional middle class can internalize an African American social and political agenda, most likely in the absence of strong social ties to the West Indian community. Under certain circumstances, this agenda may lead to African Americanization. When it does not, then the West Indian identity can acquire a sense of racialized otherness, another barrier to equal rights and justice. Under these circumstances, African Americans are perceived as champions in a perpetual racial struggle against white oppression.

Edwin McIntosh derives his West Indian identity from his deeply rooted West Indian culture. He came to the United States when he was in his mid-twenties, and his self-representation as a West Indian revolves around identific symbols, performance, and cultural rituals:

> It's a cultural thing. We still, and I think this is the same for all immigrants, same for Spanish, they would go to the Spanish club, do salsa. You've got the West Indian festivals, the carnivals, we would go to see if we [can] find a West Indian club to go party, to go listen to reggae and calypso music, rather than go to the American club. The West Indian community has a couple of clubs that you can go to. Party, listen to the type of music that came out for that year, and stuff like that. We can go to New York or Canada and go to these different carnivals, and what we do is still try to keep with our brother West Indians, the cultural ties. Oh, we still use the same slangs and talk the same way. I haven't lost my accent. I can still go back to my country and still say the same things I used to say before. The clothes, the clothes we wear. The food, the food we, it's not so much the clothes, but you can wear a flower shirt, like you are

in Florida or something like to a party. It has some palm trees on there or tropical-type shirt. The food we cook is the same ethnic food that we have at home, that we cook at home. We haven't lost that. We cook that sometimes. It was a hard thing to transition from what we used to eat back home to sandwiches. What's sandwiches? What am I going to do with pizza, but it took years before we started doing that, but we still go back to it.

Before immigrating to the United States, Edwin was prominent in his country of origin as one of its top athletes. He represented his country throughout the world and was rewarded for it at home. In this way, he was able to overcome a background of impoverishment and move up in the public sector, with numerous promotions offered as rewards for the honor he brought to the nation. He came to the United States in 1976 as a legal immigrant and immediately enrolled in school:

I went straight into college, so I went to college from 1977 to 1983. So, I was pretty lucky. More so lucky than other West Indians who had come, and just started. But all of my paperwork and everything for school was prepared for me before I even got here.

Edwin eventually earned a graduate degree in a technical discipline. When visiting one of his friends who had moved to California, he was attracted by the possibilities it offered for a better "quality of life." Even though he had managed to obtain quite a good job in New York's public sector, he was disappointed with its social and economic rewards:

When I graduated, I worked for the city of New York. I was still living in Queens; it was a mixed neighborhood, but the apartments were pretty expensive, but they weren't that livable. So, when I came out here, it was nice out here. The quality of life was so different. The place was much cleaner. You didn't get roaches and mice and all that kind of stuff in apartments.

Edwin got a professional position in his area of technical expertise and quickly moved up the ladder to head a department in one of the major companies in Northern California. In the process, he became an outspoken advocate of racial justice and racial equality. Edwin's understanding of the United States is racialized; he sees racism raising "its ugly head every single day." White supremacy is at the base of the American organization, and perpetual racial struggle is the only way to resolve it. As such, he makes little distinction between the conditions of

African Americans and those of West Indians. Both communities suffer the injustices of American racism. In his recollections of New York, the two communities are collapsed into one:

> New York is a rough town. Brooklyn, Bronx, Queens, it was rough. The apartments were dirty. In New York, where the blacks and West Indians were located, all the white folks have moved away to Long Island and stuff like that, bought houses and sold the dilapidated houses to the black people and the immigrants. They bought what they left. And people are fighting for the scraps.

Thus, Edwin sees very little benefit to being West Indian. While he acknowledges some degree of white preference for West Indians, he attributes this to whites' efforts to divide and rule:

> In New York, the white professors, white employees in the college used to always say, "Oh, you West Indians are very different from the black Americans." At that time, they took us as an ally. You see? Because at the time, the black American was still fighting very hard for racial equality. They were still trying to get into their neighborhoods. They were still trying to get their jobs. It wasn't a fight with the West Indians, it was a fight with the black Americans, so every time white folks in this country got into a fight, the racism is not with the Asians or the Latinos or West Indians, it's a fight with black Americans, African Americans. And so they look for allies. "Oh, we treat you, we treat these guys better these West Indians better." See, they are going to school, they are working and they got night jobs and they do like we are doing and they are going to school. But if that West Indian tried to take that white American job, then you would become like the African Americans. Once you are below their status, once you are not a threat, as soon as the perception is that there is a threat, then they turn against you. It's happening all the time.

Edwin considers white racism to be even worse when it is directed at foreigners, so he sees West Indians as particularly vulnerable. He thinks that whites disrespect West Indians because of their accent:

> They make fun of it. They make fun of anybody who has got, who speaks in an accent or a different language, similar to them. People who are bilingual. You know they have all kinds of things they talk about, the jokes they make about you. But, you try not to let that bother you, because you got your own goals and objectives in mind, however minimal that might be. And you find that given the knowledge of all the things that are happening, as a West Indian, you know you are fighting an uphill battle to get to where they are, and you've got to just keep your head

together and pool your resources just to stay, competitive is not the word, but for want of a better word, stay competitive and to get ahead.

As a result, Edwin is very sensitive to racial insults, especially those directed at his West Indian sensibilities. He is absolutely intolerant of racism, and like his fellow African American advocates for racial justice, he uses the system to seek redress. In this regard, he has chosen to follow African Americans in the pursuit and protection of his civil rights: "If I'm on the job, and anybody pulled crap, I'm going to sue them or file charges against them." In the interview, he recounted an incident to demonstrate his approach to racial slight and injustice, in which he reveals his affinity and familiarity with African Americans:

> One white American in a meeting used to tell me, "Oh, Edwin is going to summarize what we said in [the language of his country of origin]." I sued him. So, the reason why I sued him and the way I work, is because when he was doing that, and he was saying Edwin was going to summarize in [his native language], he was demeaning me and the job I was doing. He was making a correlation between my work product and my accent. There are some folks who make a distinction or make fun of my accent in a loving manner. As I would toward a black American say, "Hey, what's up nigger?" You know, stuff like that. I don't mean that, that's just colloquial language between us. And we understand that. "Nigger, you lying." You know, that kind of stuff. So, he wasn't doing that, and he was correlating my work product with my accent and the subject of that whole thing was I couldn't do the work because I had an accent.

Edwin believes that racism profoundly affects both West Indians and African Americans and that there is no escape for West Indians:

> I don't think they [whites] distinguish between what they want to tell you. For example, if you walk down the street in San Francisco, you can identify an Asian American, you can identify a Latino, but you can't identify a West Indian from an American black unless you start talking to them and hear the accent, you see? So for that to happen and for you to make that distinction, you have to recognize that this person is a West Indian. You would not be able to recognize and would not be able to make those kinds of allegations if you just look at people in a building . . . it has to be some interaction. And compared to American blacks, Asian Americans and Latinos in this country, West Indians are a small minority, very, very small minority.

Despite Edwin's racialized understanding of America and his sympathies, he subscribes to the negative popular images of African Americans. This is typical of the West Indian middle class. Edwin believes that African Americans hold similarly negative and hostile attitudes toward West Indians, as do whites. But he sees these attitudes as stemming from a genuine concern with their economic well-being. Nonetheless, he believes that racism has produced fundamental flaws in the African American psyche that hinder their upward mobility, since they feed the tendency not to seek the opportunities that have proved so successful for West Indians:

> It's not racism. To me, their attitude toward West Indian is mostly economical, because they perceive West Indians are here to take their jobs. And most West Indians, when they get to this country, they take the jobs that Americans don't want to do, the black American don't want to do. I don't know if I should say this, but to me, some black Americans would rather be on welfare than accept certain jobs that the West Indians take. So, the discrimination between whites and blacks are different. The whites, they discriminate against you because of the color of your skin. The black Americans discriminate against you because of economic reasons. They figure you are taking away the little opportunities they have. Or any minority, anybody with an accent.

Edwin's attitudes toward race were formed by the Civil Rights movement and his own interpretation of its effect on the opportunities made available to black West Indians:

> My general impression of black Americans is that they went through so much in this country in terms of being slaves and the kind of treatment they got, they suffered. I feel that they suffered for me, for you, for every other minority in this country. They suffered terribly. They fought for what we are getting now. When I went to college, it was because of what African Americans did. What Martin Luther King did. What all the other, Jesse Jackson, all the other leaders, what they did. And they did that for every other ethnic immigrant, minority in this country. Latinos, everybody. They got beaten, they got kicked on, and my general impression of them is, they are a tough people. If it wasn't for them, I wouldn't have been here today. I would not have had a college education, I would not have had a good job, because I wouldn't have been let in the door. They paved the way for me. So, my impression of them is that they fought a good fight and they helped me to be where I am.

Edwin's professional life takes precedence over his social affinities, which partly explains his participation in the American discourse of race. His attitudes are influenced less by the social network of West Indians and more by the realities of his occupational and professional position. Edwin claims very weak social ties to the West Indian community. Indeed, he has both West Indian and American acquaintances but no "really close friends." Edwin explained his involvement with West Indians in cultural terms and considers his social life to be very "limited." He goes to West Indian functions, dances, and cultural activities:

> I guess there is, distinguishable, you got acquaintances, you got friends and you got, I don't think I've got great, great friends that I can trust with my life and that kind of stuff. Here, you don't have a lot of time for it. You are so much on the go to get and achieve certain things, that, that becomes secondary. Friendship is a luxury that comes from you having a lot of spare time. Even though you may have spare time in the sense of the word, like you can, like you're home Saturday, Sunday, stuff like that, you are always on the go. Some people take work home. They don't want to be bothered, you call some people, "Hey, you want to do this?" "No, I got things to do."
>
> I have acquaintances, some of them are West Indians, some are Americans, like I say, they are not great friends that I go over to their house and have dinner and they come to my house and have dinner and the kids sleep here.

What emerges in Edwin's self-representations are the intertwining of a West Indian identity understood and defined in cultural terms and a black identity that takes its cues from his own understanding of the history and current conditions facing the African American professional. This understanding is based on the same civil rights agenda that informs the African American access to opportunity. Edwin's weak involvement in social networks has prevented the absorption of immigrant understandings of African Americans as reflected in West Indian middle-class opinion. Edwin thus has been able to maintain a sense of his own West Indianness despite his involvement in the sociopolitical agenda of the African American community: "Even though I'm an American citizen, I still consider myself a West Indian. When anyone asks 'Where are you from?' I don't say I'm an American. I say I am West Indian. No problem with that, that ain't a problem whatsoever." At the same time, Edwin describes himself as an American when the issue relates to politics: "I kind of gave up my country right now, instead of, in terms of being involved in its politics and where they want to go, and this and that. You can say, literally, I'm an American. I'm into the American politics. I vote American. I do everything American right now." So it is in his political and legal engagement with the system that Edwin identifies most with African Americans. At the same time, in his imagination the cultural consequences of racism have damaged the African American psyche. It is in this latter representation that Edwin reflects typically stereotypical understandings of African Americans. Although he mentions heroes of the racial and civil rights struggle, he never speaks of African American successes in other arenas.

Roy Gillette

When a deep sense of West Indian cultural identity is reinforced by exclusive involvement in West Indian social networks, it may lead to social isolation from the African American professional and occupational system of support. This can limit opportunities for upward mobility despite professional qualification unless alternatives can be found through the West Indian network

Roy Gillette comes from a background of social and economic privilege. He followed what is considered to be the "normal" trajectory of immigration for someone from his socioeconomic circle with expectations of further education and professional opportunities:

> In terms of furthering your education, from a small island like that, the United States was the place most people came to. The United States was the place that most people—some people pick Canada. Some people pick the U.K. In my situation, I picked—well, my parents picked the United States because I had family here that I could reside with until I was able to stand on my own. So that was the main reason because I had family here that could look out for my well-being initially.

He describes opportunities available in his island home to be confined "basically to tourism and crops." So the island's elite was expected to immigrate. Roy saw his residence in the United States almost as an extension of his life of privilege in his country of origin. His social network of friends remained confined to those in the small age-cohort with whom he had bonded almost from birth. They all had immigrated to the United

States within a year of one another to join already established extensions of their own families:

> It just happened that way because of our—we graduated from high school about the same time. They were around my age group, and they were in the same standard or same form. So, yeah, so we left there about the same time because most of—most of their parents had someone in the United States in which they came up and stayed with, or they had family. Most seemed to have some family or some connection in the United States, which made it easier to come to the United States.

Roy immigrated as a legal permanent resident, as his nuclear family had been sponsored by an uncle:

> I was legal because I had an uncle that filed for my whole family to get our green card. So I came here and got my green card. I went through the process of going through [my country of origin] to the U.S. consulate [there]. I got my green card a few months after arriving here. So everything in my case was legal. I had family. I had family that lived here for a number of years that was able to sponsor me.

Roy enrolled in a university in the Washington, D.C., area while staying with family members who were living in Maryland. His decision was determined by the quality of life in Maryland compared with that in New York. What remains unspoken is that in making this decision, Roy was able to retain the exclusivity of his social position by remaining separated from the less privileged and less well-off New York West Indian community:

> I had family in New York, and I had family in Maryland, and I chose—we chose Maryland because the environment in Maryland was considered better by my family that lived in Maryland over New York. I think New York, having a reputation as it always has of a big city, and it—and the crime, and all the things that go with a big city, they figured that Maryland was a better atmosphere. Out of the city, out of the big city.

After graduating with a degree in engineering and working for a time in New York, Roy got a job at a "start-up" company in Northern California. The opportunity to join the company was provided by one of his small cohort of friends from childhood, who was one of its vice-presidents. Roy sees these personal connections as essential to success:

> I think part of it has to do with whom you know. I think it pays off if you know somebody in the position that's able to help you. If you know

somebody in a position that's able to help you, which happened in my case, then that's all you need, that big break, and then if you—one thing can lead to the other. Because I came out here, it was a temporary job. I was offered a temporary job. I came out here, and I stayed with him for a few months. The job was six months temporary, with a possibility of being permanent, but then I had decided what I have to do.

Roy subscribes to notions of meritorious success, once an opportunity is made available:

And when I came out here, my first emphasis was to show them I could do the job and to become permanent. And I did that three months after I started the job. They made me permanent. Yeah. They wanted to see if I could—if I was worthy of doing the job with my education, I guess, and all of these factors. So yes, I guess I had to demonstrate that yes, my—I could do what the job demands, and after three months, they made me permanent, so that was the first step. Then after that, after they made me permanent. I showed them that I could do the job, and so they made me permanent, and that was my first step toward relocating.

Soon the start-up was acquired by a major company and expanded, thereby securing Roy's professional and socioeconomic success. His understanding of his own success is based on a combination of the reciprocal obligations of friendship, merit, and the fortuitous circumstances of the company's acquisition. This understanding is different from the types of racial consciousness that can emerge from involvement with and dependence on the African American professional and occupational network. Roy developed strong and exclusive bonds with his elite circle of childhood friends both in the United States and back home. He avoided all other types of social affinities:

Most of the socializing I do is with my friends that I grew up with. They were my neighbors back in my home country. So these are people that I grew up with all my life so—and I have four of them so those are the people that I'm mostly socializing with here. I haven't socialized with Americans here, and I haven't—only the people on my job, and they're of such mixed nature—Filipinos and so forth, and I can't really comment on them because it's just a working relationship. The people that I keep in touch with from the Caribbean are my friends that I knew from my high-school days, and I have a lot of them over here, and there's some that I've met from all my years of being over here. So those are the people that I keep in touch with because I've known them from being over here so long, and we met in different social gatherings, and through—this friend, they know that person, and so forth. So I have quite a few friends over here that I keep in touch with. Other than that, other than those people that I've known for years, I really haven't socialized that much in terms of meeting people.

Roy sees his own accomplishments almost as part of the "natural order" for those in his own social position. He describes his friends exclusively in terms of their own achievements:

Once they left home, and they came to this country, they got degrees. My four friends here, for example, the four people that I know here, one has a master's. He's a hydrogeologist. The other one is a vice-president—the one that I work with is vice-president of manufacturing. He has a master's in chemical engineering. The other guy—it's three guys, one works with me. The other one is a mechanical engineer. Most of my friends I still associate with have degrees. One of my closest female friends over here, she's a lawyer. She's a public defender on the East Coast.

Roy's sense of his own accomplishment as preordained by his social position combined with notions of social privilege to form his attitude toward race and African Americans. This attitude also is affected by the class attitudes in his country of origin, which he retains, and are reinforced in his current pattern of social relations. He believes that a lower-class background is a source of shame and embarrassment:

Some people leave my country of origin, and they don't even—some people probably wouldn't admit that that's where they're from, or that's where they were brought up. I think some people hide the fact that—some people hide where they're from. Some people just choose to—hate to identify with things of the past especially if it wasn't pleasant, or if it kind of degrades them. I think to some people, the lifestyle they grew up with back home was so much of a lower class than here to them that they may suppress it.

In contrast, Roy presents his own class background as one to be envied. "For the most part, Americans are very intrigued when they realize that the lifestyle that I grew up with—that's the lifestyle in the way I grew up. I am in a different class." This is the source of his own superiority, even to Americans, and of his West Indian identity:

Because most Americans that I have dealt with, they just seem very intrigued as to the culture, the way in which I was brought up, and the things that we did because they just found—they found that—I mean my thoughts and ideas were so much different to them, to Americans. I guess, Americans, they associate people probably in my age group, they found that my intellectual level seemed a bit higher than people of my age group in the United States. So they were always intrigued and always curious, always wanted to know more about the Island, the way of life, what we did, how did we live. I think they were, for the most part, they were always curious as to ask about it. That's what I found, they were always curious about the lifestyle of people who live on islands.

Because of his sense of West Indian privilege, Roy sees no distinction between himself and whites. He emphasizes his background, from which notions of race were absent:

I grew up in a country where there's—yeah, there's white people, but I never realized that there was such a big difference in the color until I came to this country. Because I went to school with kids that were white, and it never occurred to me. And if you ask my friends here, it never occurred to you. You sat beside someone in high school that was white, and you never—I never realized it until I came to this country the way you really see such a big difference between black and whites. It never occurred to me while I was growing up as a child. So I always look—I always look past that racial, and I always look past color lines. I don't think I'm denied something because I was black.

His views also affect Roy's attitude toward African Americans, which is deeply rooted in his own sense of privilege. He believes that they "envy the lifestyle that we—in the most part, they envy the lifestyle that I had." Roy also believes that African Americans and other minorities use race as a crutch and an excuse for their own failure:

I think race relations—I think they try to bring race into so many things. They try to bring race into so many things that I think you'd be better off leaving race alone. Just in so many things, they make race such a big thing. I think there's quite a bit of them that once they cannot achieve something that they want to achieve, or they've been set back in some specific area, that think it's racism. People just have to change their whole attitude.

For Roy, character and merit are the bases of success:

I think a lot of it has to do with character. Character. The character of a person. I think it's the most powerful thing. And I think a lot of people treat you putting race and color and all of that aside, I think the character and your level of education. I think that stands out more than anything else. I think if you have a strong personality, and you have a good head on your shoulders, I think you probably—I think you'll fit into any situation.

Clearly, Roy believes that these two qualities are responsible for his success in the United States, and as a result, he claims never to have been discriminated against.

Roy's class background and attitudes are implicated in his racial attitudes. He managed to bring his sense of class superiority with him to the United States and to maintain it by strongly identifying with his sociocultural background as a West Indian. By keeping his social ties to his class peers and cohort, he was able to insulate himself from the American racial discourse, and he used the reciprocal obligations of his class position to achieve his professional success. In turn, his success has given Roy independence from the professional and occupational network of the African American middle class. Because there is absolutely no reason to activate his blackness, he has developed an identity devoid of race and justifies it in terms of a background of racial equality.

Discourses on Blackness

Whether or not race is a problem, the attitudes of West Indians in Northern California toward African Americans have been formed from a deep and ubiquitous sense of social and cultural difference, sustained by the pervasive social construction of the immigrant as a permanent foreigner. At the individual level, the West Indian identity in Northern California is predicated on the person's participatory experiences in the country of origin and his or her social interpretations and memories of them. Besides being shaped by the social geography of the San Francisco Bay Area, these experiences combine with images of West Indians in the American popular consciousness to differentiate them from African Americans. Race is at the center of these distinctions. At one extreme, African Americans are distinguished by their use of race as a crutch and an excuse for failure and underachievement. This is the view of those whose West Indian identity does not include blackness as a problem. At the other extreme, African Americans are presented as victims of racism and as so affected by racial struggle as to damage their character and take away some of their humanity. This is the view of those whose experiences and understandings include a fundamental sense of their own black identity. For these people, even their shared blackness is not enough to create a common identity with African Americans.

However notions of difference are represented, they reflect the stereotypical white portrayal of African Americans as "cold," "hostile" "loud," "lazy," and "envious." There is a general sense that these attitudes and character traits are responsible for the division between African Americans and West Indians, with many West Indians believing that the fault rests with the former. Sometimes they see African Americans' hostility as related to their perception of West Indians and West Indians' success.

> The black Americans to a certain extent think that the West Indians think that they are better off. That we come here to talk to white people only, or we think we are much smarter, or we come and work for smaller wages, and eventually we acquire homes. And there's some resentment to all that.

Many West Indians attribute these attitudes not to African American perceptions but to West Indians' actual achievements and to envy:

> African Americans always think that we've come over here to take the money. And every time they tell me that, I say "Exactly. You don't like to go to school, and you don't like to work. So I'll come and I'll take it." They don't really like me, the people that I know.

Some West Indians attribute African Americans' hostility to their belief that West Indians have never had to struggle:

> They have this chip-on-the-shoulder thing, and I found some jealousy between the black Americans, the African Americans, and the West Indians because somehow they felt that you didn't have the hardships that they had. You didn't go through the racism or whatever it was that they went through.

Underlying all this is a genuine sense of historical difference that many attribute to different experiences of racism and slavery:

> Some African Americans will say, "You guys have it much easier because your slavery wasn't as harsh as our slavery." Or, "You, although you had slavery, it might have been harsh, but you were all together. We are scattered here."

The following respondent addressed more explicitly the idea of a different history and its consequences:

> I think African Americans had a really hard life. I think as West Indians we didn't really understand what they went through. And you know, when I first came here, I would hear if the American, black American,

would apply themselves, they would have much more for themselves. And as I delved into their history more, I realized that we're a little more fortunate in the Caribbean. We're from the same African slaves. But we were a lot more fortunate. I think black Americans are just beginning to really find themselves, and that the struggle that they've gone through, we're much more lucky coming from the smaller islands, and its not all their fault for the situation they're in today.

In sum, most West Indians recognize the significance of white perceptions in their own distinctions between West Indians and African Americans. As a result, the differences between the two are contextualized in terms of white understanding and white sensibilities: "White Americans realize the difference. Now, West Indians, they know they have something to do, they are going to do it. And that's it. I find black Americans, now, they have something to do, they have to, they will take their time, do what they have to do, but mixing stuff with it."

Many respondents thought that whites were more apt to accept and preferred West Indians because of their familiarity with West Indian culture through travel and education:

> White Americans are definitely interested in my culture and knowing about it and I would say the more educated a person was, they were a little bit more knowledgeable about the Caribbean and different parts of the world. And so we could carry on a little bit more conversation about it and do a little more exchange.

> As far as White Americans, I think they understand us even more than African Americans. They may have some sort of prejudice against blacks, they tend to treat us with a little more respect.

Because of whites' distinctions between West Indians and African Americans, some respondents saw a disadvantage in adopting an African American identity:

> Once whites understand that you are foreign, that acknowledgment lends itself toward you as a matter of fact to be viewed differently. If as a West Indian, you adopt the American accent and the American cultural norms, you definitely will be viewed as a black American.

While acknowledging their own blackness, many respondents believed that white Americans did not consider them to be black. Even though the perception of not being black was considered by all to be desirable, a few respondents expressed surprise and shock at the discovery:

It was traumatic for me, you know. I was not aware of the impact of it, but I'm sure that it did have an impact on how people viewed me. Over the years, I have realized that yes, people think that you're something else. You're not black. I've had people tell me this. I was working at this place, and I said, "I'm going to the Bay Area Black United Fund. They're having a big dinner and stuff." They said, "You're not black." "What do you think I am?" It was like, "Well, what does she perceive me to be?" I just didn't get it.

Almost all the respondents agreed that their difference from African Americans was firmly rooted in the social, cultural, and political circumstances of their West Indian background:

A West Indian because we have been ourselves leaders of our countries, just of our own fate after colonialism and getting our own independence, we have become accustomed to seeing our own black people in charge. Some of us left situations where we were in charge and in high prominence in our country. That is not the experience for many of the black Americans whom I have met. And so the West Indian can approach a situation with a certain degree of confidence, with a little degree of "Gee, we have had a long history of associating with white folks and dealing with them. We don't have to leave them to do everything." A certain degree of tolerance, a certain degree of being able to rest something aside and let it be. Whereas, the black Americans, these things are more volatile, they are more likely to react to them because that's their experience.

The West Indian experience of black agency explained to many respondents the different attitudes of African Americans and West Indians:

Even though there was slavery in Jamaica, we were in the majority. And Jamaica is 90 percent black. Even though you can find all different shades in Jamaica, the fact of the matter is, Jamaicans do not have an inferiority complex. We never had that. And one of the big things, big differences that you notice is difference in attitude. And that's why a lot of people say, "Oh, West Indians, they're too arrogant." And that's a big difference. Because we certainly don't believe anybody's better than us. And we don't believe anybody owes us anything or anything like that. So that's probably the main difference. There's a difference in that.

None of this means that West Indians are not conscious of racism at least as an issue in American life. A few respondents, however, discounted its effects altogether, seeing it as an excuse and a crutch:

America will give you what you put into it. In the midst of all its problems, be it unfair treatment to minorities—if you present yourself and you package everything about you right, America will not bother with you. So the excuse that the white man, all of this is to oppress the black man, I find that to be a lame excuse for the lazy and those who don't want to get up and work. I truly find that, because there is a place for everyone in America.

A few respondents criticized this tendency to be oblivious to the consequences of racism and to its negative consequences for black people. But they attributed these attitudes to the nuances of its manifestation that could camouflage the existence of racism.

Yeah, I think there is racism here, but I think it's very subtle. And I think they try to pretend that it isn't here, but it's very much so. I think it's just sad because we're living a lie that there's not a lot of racism here for us, and there really is. And we have to open up our eyes and see it.

One respondent suggested that the West Indian middle class may not be in the best position to judge its effect:

It's a game, and only in the inner cities is there the reality, do you see the reality of what's happening? The rest of it is like a game. Race relations is just a game. I think essentially, white people don't like black people, and the sooner white people get to realize that, it's fine. I believe that until the end of time, whites have a supernationalist attitude, and they feel that they're better than everybody else, and that's not going to change.

Another respondent attributed the tendency to discount or minimize the existence of racism to the "colonial mentality" that West Indians bring as part of their cultural baggage to the United States:

Maybe because we're a little colonized—I don't necessarily think that's my attitude. But maybe in some cases we sort of look up to the white man. I don't know how true that is. But there may be some truth in that.

Many respondents described racism as a mere inconvenience to be tolerated:

I always heard about discrimination, but I never experienced it because, truthfully, I'm the kind of person that I look at an individual not by the color or the race, but by the individual that they are, and in this incident I was shopping off Canal Street in the city. And we stopped to get—I think we stopped for a beer, and we went into this little pub, and it was me and a lady. And there was a Caucasian lady sitting next to us. And I didn't hear the remark at first. And the lady said, did you hear her con-jecture? I said no. But then she even repeated it herself, and then they heard it. She said, "These black niggers all over the place." The owner or bartender, the owner even complained at that time, and they actually threw her out of the pub, the place, that day. But I have never experi-enced anything like that anymore.

With a very few exceptions, the respondents who acknowledged racism as a problem represented it in interpersonal terms with which they could deal as individuals:

I try to deal with each incident individually. As it happens I deal with it. I do whatever is necessary. I make whatever complaints. I write letters at a flash. And get satisfaction, what satisfaction is available.

And from another respondent:

I had a patient who was white, and she came back the following year for an examination. She had mentioned to her primary-care physician that I had seen her and that I was very professional; however, she did not want me touching her, because I was black. And her primary-care physician with whom I had a professional relationship thought that the smartest thing to do in that case was that I should not attend to her, because I am black and she doesn't want it. So I should not do it. And I didn't think that was fair. Because I felt that he should have stopped it right there. And he didn't. He should have said, "Well, you know [this HMO] hires people based on their educational background and not their race, be-cause I had to do a lot of studying to reach to this point. But instead he wrote a note saying I should not do her examination. And it got out of hand, and the HMO wrote her a letter telling her that if she wasn't pleased with their decision to have me do her examination, then she should find another health-care [provider].

These two accounts highlighted a particular tendency among West Indians when dealing with racial incidents. They view racism as an in-dividual problem that can be addressed institutionally, for the system is always on the side of racial justice, which is its saving grace. Many felt that they were quite capable of handling racism:

I'm very conscious about who I am, what I'm about. The issues sur-rounding racism, the problems, I can't let that hinder me. I have to get beyond that. And even though the system dictates that you can't even get a loan for your business, I have to figure out a way how to get around that. Rather than sitting back and saying, "This is the system." Even if you are on welfare, I think you can use the system, as far as I can see sometimes to your advantage to get out, do things.

There is a sense of efficacy in dealing with the problems of racism and racial discrimination exhibited among those West Indian respondents who have experienced its effects personally:

> I've been meeting with other black parents at our kids' high school to get a staff development day to deal with racism, and that started as the result of a racial incident at the school. Some little punk kid wrote in the underground newspaper some things about certain kids who sit on the bench. The bench is where all the black kids and Hispanic kids hang out. And you know, he made some really stereotypical remarks, and that got the whole school in an uproar. And you know, the parents started to meet, and we came up with this idea that this kind of stuff would not—this kid would not have thought to put that there if he didn't think that there was a climate, you know, that existed that would accept that. So we thought, "Well, we should start with the teachers and, you know, move on." And it did happen. The staff development day. And we just designed a whole day around talking about how things affect our kids and stuff. So that, that type of thing, if something affects your kids, you always get involved. So it's trying to make the school a better place for kids.

Some respondents felt that the way to deal with racism was to ignore it: "I don't get angry, I just figure they don't know better. I just ignore them." Another respondent said, "There are times when I just walk away, and there are times when I just look at a person and say, 'I really pity you for your ignorance. I really feel sorry for you that you can't see me as another human being.'"

In the words of a third:

> When it comes to race, I'm a bit on the naive side. I try to block it out. I don't really look for it. I don't think about it. I have seen. I have heard, but I don't spend that much time worrying about it because all it does, it just basically keeps you back. I am not into allowing someone else to dictate my life, what I should and should not do.

For the most part, the West Indian respondents feel detached from the problems of racism. While acknowledging its presence, many claim that it has not affected them or that they cannot recall any incidences of discrimination and prejudice. A few saw racism and discrimination as inevitable and part of the natural order:

Every nation oppresses their own. Every culture you go in the world by definition oppresses their own. There is no culture in the world that's free of being oppressed by your own people.

Other respondents accepted it with a degree of fatalism:

I had been at this job for a really long time, and I thought, "Oh, I'm working my way up because of hard work." But you can work really hard and not succeed basically because you are black. So it doesn't really matter if you're West Indian. In the end, it doesn't matter if you're a West Indian or an American. I see that very clearly. You're still black, you know.

Similarly:

I think that life in America, it's a race thing. It's a race thing because if you're not black, you're white. And if you're not white, you're alien. If you're not black, you're alien.

Some of the respondents used the issue of racism to condemn what is almost universally felt in the West Indian community as rejection by African Americans:

On the job, I want to kick them, it was all African American. They were part—like I said, they would make fun of us and tell us to go back on the ship. To go back to where we came from.

According to another respondent,

I have experienced prejudice and hostility from black Americans who actually accuse me of taking their jobs, and I say, "We're not even in the same field. What are you talking about?" "Well, you come here and take jobs at a cheaper rate." And that was directed at me because I was from the Caribbean.

Some respondents saw African American prejudice as part of a generalized and pervasive anti-immigrant attitude of intolerance in America.

I experience prejudice from Americans on the whole. If you say, "Oh my gosh, I don't like this, or why they have to do it like that." And if you made the mistake and said, "Oh, in my country it's not done like that." Both Americans, white and black, would say, "Well, go back to where you're from." So you have to be real careful what you say around these Americans.

Whatever the point of view and whatever the perspective, the West Indian respondents believed that their uniqueness placed them above the American racial discourse, protected them from its consequences, or provided them with the means of adjusting to it.

> One thing that I don't like to do is generalize too much because I have learned that, of course, each person is different. There are some folks that I see, at times, are intimidated by us because, yes, we are able to identify with the racism and all of those stereotypes that are in place in this country. . . . Although we can identify and empathize with the black Americans, me, personally, I really wasn't into race as much as I see a lot of my black American friends are into it and are intimidated by it. They have strong feelings about it. I kind of like was on the outside looking in. I could understand it, empathize with it, but I am not involved. I've never experienced it. I don't know if I can say I put on my blinders, but I really don't look for it. I just go ahead and do what I am hired to do, I was paid to do. That has been my approach for years.

Some see their socioeconomic status as protecting them from the effects of racism:

> Let me tell you something—and my friends sometimes don't agree with me—I've had no problems with racism, no problem at all. I don't know. It may have to do with how I carry myself, my profession, my education. I have never had any problems with that.

Conclusion

Collectively and individually, West Indians in Northern California negotiate their location in the social construction of American difference by activating a collective conscience of themselves as permanent foreigners and as successful. These understandings of West Indians are accommodated in the geosocial context of Northern California to which foreigners can legitimately claim to belong and where West Indian migratory patterns discriminate in favor of a professional and educated elite. The social construction of West Indians as upwardly mobile, meritocratic, and foreign supports cognitive distinctions that differentiate them from African Americans. Indeed, these distinctions are used to support claims that West Indians are "not black." When blackness is acknowledged in self-representations, it is constructed in ways that lack the negative stereotypes that exist in the white imagination. This allows West Indians in Northern California to retain their sense of racial distinction while holding on to notions of American blackness that reflect the popular white consciousness. West Indians see themselves as either existing above the racial discourse or as possessing the moral and characterological means to overcome its consequences. They see themselves as amenable to the white embrace and white understanding in ways that African Americans are not and can never be. This has to do with their West Indianness and the way that their participatory experiences allow the positive accommodation of difference. In their own self-conceptualizations, West Indians are masters of their fate in ways that African Americans are not. They are able to see racism for what it is and not let its consequences control their lives. Their very success insulates them, in their own self-understandings, from its consequences.

These understandings and self-representations of West Indianness in the San Francisco Bay Area could not be sustained without the objective conditions of socioeconomic success, which is why access to the West Indian community and claims to West Indianness are so restricted to the upwardly mobile. They explain the pressures on individuals to achieve and also why the process of African Americanization or American ethnicization has failed to take root in the West Indian community. The former comes with the inevitability of entering the African American community, and successful West Indians see such identification as undesirable and harmful. American ethnicization is produced in the context of political competition for resources of citizenship by communities identified by their geographic concentrations. These communities are usually sustained by common socioeconomic interests. No such community of West Indians exists in California, nor is there a basis for it given the divergent interests of West Indians.

What is invisible in the social construction of West Indians is the dependence of their success in Northern California on a system of race relations shaped by the social and political power of African Americans. West Indians can remain "above the fray" because their racial interests have been secured by civil rights protection and by the access this provides to opportunities for upward mobility. This is the basis of the West Indians' ambiguous attitudes toward African Americans. For many West Indians, the history of racism and racial struggle in America has taken a toll on African Americans' morality and psyche. It is this history that distinguishes West Indians from African Americans. West Indians' status as permanent foreigners emerges from a history that is definitively not American. So there is little need for successful West Indians in Northern California to identify with the racial struggle of African Americans. To do so, they would have to identify publicly as African Americans, and this would be incompatible with their self-conceptualizations of achievement and with their self-definitions as permanent foreigners.

6

Constructing an Immigrant Identity

Notions of a Permanent Foreigner

Sociologist Paul Gilroy (1997) speaks of "a distinctive ecology of belonging" in reference to understandings of self that relate to immigration. Among the most pervasive features of modernity is the association between territoriality and identity and between territorial sovereignty and belonging. The latter two—ultimately translated into notions of citizenship—became the basis of claims to rights and assertions of privilege. The roots of modernity were planted in the transoceanic movement of persons. Dislocation demanded definite notions of belonging. New understandings tied these notions to bounded territory, and obligations to territory produced expectations of return. The growing disjunction between location of residence and location of origin produced longings for return, marking the beginning of a diasporic imagination. In the fragmented geographies of new diasporic locations, new notions of original territory were born, couched in terms of a fatherland or motherland. Cultural constructions of territories of belonging were imprinted on an uprooted progeny. Longings for return persisted, fed by images of home and tempered by neither distance nor time.

West Indian identity in Northern California is negotiated, accommodated, and ultimately located in the socially constructed space of the immigrant. And the immigrant is popularly imagined as a permanent foreigner with a legitimate claim of belonging. This legitimacy in California's geoeconomy, in turn, is derived from the immigrant's perceived role in the popular imagination. Permanent foreigners and legitimate immigrants are believed to provide the skills and education needed in the technology- and knowledge-based industries that drive California's economy.

In its cognitive construction, the idea of the permanent foreigner is incompatible with notions of national identity. The rights of residence and of identity are different, with the latter understood in terms of diasporic origin. These distinctions produce an identific detachment from American nationalist constructs of belonging.

The distinction between the right of belonging based on residence and the right of national identity based on origin muddies the meaning of the permanent immigrant's presence in the host country. It emerges in the interpretations provided by permanent foreigners of their presence on American soil. America becomes the country in which they happen to reside for practical and specific reasons that have very little to do with a desire to become an "American." This, of course, contradicts the "melting pot" myth of national absorption that exists in the American popular imagination.

Permanent foreigners find numerous ways to rationalize their residence in the United States. Their continued allegiance to their countries of origin is supported and defended in moral, ethical, social, cultural, and even economic narratives of national superiority. West Indians in Northern California use such narratives in their self-representations, including in them tales of sacrifice and loss and claims to the desirable qualities lacking in their country of residence.

A contradiction arises when the demonstrated benefits of migration, material or otherwise, are compared with assertions of the home country's superiority. This creates a dilemma for immigrants trying to justify their continued residence in the United States. The dilemma is heightened when the immigrants' identity is organized around notions of success and achievement that inform popular understandings.

West Indians in Northern California use images of home and interpretations of the United States to create coherent narratives in their self-representations as permanent foreigners. These narratives represent their attempts to give meaning to their presence in the United States in ways that accommodate their own notions of national superiority. They select for valorization certain elements in the moral, social, cultural, political, and/or economic organization and framework of their countries of origin. In the process, the benefits derived from migration can be downgraded in the larger scheme of values. Accomplishments in the host countries can be explained in terms of the immigrants' core values that define their diasporic identity or in terms of the knowledge and skills acquired in their countries of origin. Accordingly, immigration can be presented as a net loss of fundamental values or a sacrifice of higher values.

Fantasies and Disappointments

When explaining their presence in the United States, almost all the West Indian respondents mentioned their idealistic expectations of easy wealth and abundant opportunities, generated by movies, television, and stories about America told by friends and relatives who had already immigrated. They were supported by demonstrations of abundance evident in the immigrants' possessions and the gifts that they lavished on those who remained at home. Before immigrating, the West Indian respondents thought of the United States as a fantasy. Such an impression is at the heart of America's seductiveness and is the root cause of the eventual and inevitable disappointment. The following excerpts from the accounts of seven of the respondents are typical of the understandings of America before immigration:

> We always lived with the impression that America is a very wealthy place, and everything goes good.

> It was supposed to be the land of milk and honey. You know, it's something you read about and see. It was kind of like a dream.

> I thought that America was the land where no wrong could be done, you know? You know the shows that we saw in the Caribbean, I have to admit that they showed all the good side of America. And all these showed more or less the upper hand of America, America being moralistic. You know, everybody's got a chance and all that good stuff.

> My impressions, I guess the impressions I got were basically from people who were living in the United States, and primarily went home to visit. But the things that you heard, you know, the United States was basically this great place. I mean, you basically could go over there and get rich very fast. My impression was that basically I guess you can say that probably the streets are lined with gold.

> It was the land of milk and honey. Everything, the way people talk about it, it's as if money grew on trees.

> I thought, you know, that everybody back home would see me on TV because I'm going to be a famous star. I'm going to be a famous star, and I'm going to be a model.

> It always was a dream. You know, it always seemed to be the ideal place perhaps because of what you see on the television and the movies, and it was always a dream, the ultimate place to be where all your goals can be reached, and your dreams can come true.

Identific narratives of difference between West Indians and Americans first appear in memories of the first impressions of the United States, many of which entail encounters with the culture of American blackness:

> I was disappointed because I came to—the first time I came to the United States, I went to New York. It was the first time I had seen a black majority population since I left home, and I was very disappointed by the way they reacted to us. The way blacks treated blacks in New York in the 1960s was very disappointing, and specifically the way the black Americans responded to the Caribbean culture. They were not interested at all.

> My impressions were that I would come and be around another set of African people from the diaspora, and perhaps we can work together. The impressions I had back home living around mostly Africans was that it would probably be the same when I came to the United States. But that wasn't the case. After arriving here, I realized that there's a lot of animosity between African Americans and those Africans coming from outside of America from the West Indies or from Africa.

Other narratives were of encounters with American morality and American values:

> People here, I think they are selfish, because everybody is looking out for themselves, and if somebody is taller and bigger than you, they'll just crush you and keep going, because they are trying to get somewhere. And if you don't move fast enough to get out of their way, or if you don't move fast enough to where you are going, they'll get there before you, and you'll be left out.

> The lack of freedom was one of the main concerns because as somebody—even here on holiday and after I moved up, there were always warnings from family members who lived here before about being cautious about going out on the streets.

> Though they say that this is the land of the free, they have more ordinances and more laws than anything I've ever seen in my entire life. So I am not too sure what democracy and freedom really mean, because if this is the land of the free, then my country is the land of whatever you call that which is greater than freedom.

For the most part, however, West Indian respondents expressed deep disappointment with the social, physical, and environmental conditions that they were forced to endure when they arrived. The picture they presented was of profound and potentially permanent discomfort, of suffering and loss that denied or dwarfed claims of improvement and achievement:

I was in Boston, just cold and lonely.

There were so many elements that basically kept you down that it made it even much more difficult. But it was nowhere in terms of what I had envisioned America would be like.

I didn't think that the situation for black people would be so horrendous. And it really amazed me. It was just really weird. To me, what was even more amazing was the fact that West Indian families, a lot of families that I had known, left the West Indies, left reasonably good homes and came here and lived like in these little roach-infested two-by-four apartments. That surprised me. You always get the impression that life here is better, but I couldn't see how life was any better here than it was at home. It was just a lot worse than I thought it would be. I had never envisioned gold-paved roads or whatever. But it was worse than I thought it would be.

I got off the plane, coming from a hot tropical country, coming into the winter. It was a cultural shock. I was so angry. I was angry, I was in shock. I was upset. I didn't want to talk. I think I got really, really withdrawn because I knew that it was cold, but then when I actually felt it for myself, I didn't think any place could be this cold, coming from the sun. So I wanted to go back immediately. I didn't want to stay.

I went to New York, and when I saw the place, I was totally shocked. The place was shabby and not clean and just really awful. And so I wanted to go back home immediately. You think of America as a beautiful place, land of, probably milk and honey. And then when you see the place, you are shocked. Is this the America?

America, eew, it was ugly. I was miserable, you know, coming out of the heat into the cold. And then everybody hustling. You don't have a name no more. So even if you don't give your name, most times they don't ask you for a name, they ask you for a social security number.

And it's funny. It's something that I've taken the time to really observe with West Indians. They come to this country seeking a better life. And a lot of times, they're not living a better life. They've left a more quality life at home.

I was not prepared for the racism. I had no idea it existed, even though I was a black guy. When I see someone, I see them as an equal. He's white, he's a nice guy. I did not realize that people have such great prejudices.

For a few of the respondents, California represented a refuge from the initial disappointment with the United States, as it offered the possibility of "belonging" while maintaining an identity of foreignness. The construction of an immigrant identity allows one to be separated from America while living on its soil and enjoying its benefits. One respondent evoked images of accessibility to snow and water when explaining California's desirability:

> My first impression was that it was dirty because I came by in New York, but as I traveled further to California, I suddenly realized how beautiful it was here, living here in the Bay Area. I realized that I could get to the snow. I could get to the water, and water was really important to me.

The theme of engaged separation is evident in the following reflection. It is a narrative of concerned interest that deals with the conditions of blacks from the viewpoint of an objective and sympathetic observer, an expression of separateness tinged with concern. This is typical of the way in which West Indians in Northern California deal with the contradictions of their blackness:

> I came here in 1968 when all the black power movement was really coming up, and they were making strides. Things were really, you know, hopeful for black people at that time. And a lot of them were getting educated, and I remember also it was the time of—all kinds of things were happening. I just felt like a spectator. And it was like, "Hey, let me sit back and watch the show." I never did the things that kids were caught up in because I always felt like an outsider, like a spectator.

These impressions of the United States reveal the cognitive strategies that West Indians use to resolve the contradictions inherent in their status as permanent foreigners. How do they explain their presence in the United States and their decision to leave a country that they now idealize as superior? How can their narratives of hardship, disappointment, and loss be reconciled with their choice to live permanently in the United States? The West Indian immigrants seem to be saying that America's seductiveness precluded a rational and objective appraisal of its reality until it was too late. Otherwise, they may have chosen to remain at home.

Of all the respondents, only two held more nuanced and less idealistic impressions of the United States before they arrived. Both had spent a number of years in Great Britain and had moved directly from there to Northern California. It was clear that the issue of race was paramount in their earlier impressions and that it was shaped by their British experiences. Both explained that they did not plan to move to the United States. Contained in the details are their rationalizations for choosing to live in the United States. As exceptions to the narrative of seduction, their self-representations shed considerable light on the West Indian construction of identities as permanent foreigners.

Elizabeth Hartley

As the light-complexioned daughter of "very affluent" parents, Elizabeth Hartley recounted a life of privilege in the color/class hierarchy of her country of origin. Her move to Great Britain represented a loss of status in the racial order. She may have combined her prior exposure to racism, loss of racial status, and marriage to an African American in the recollections of her impressions of the United States before coming here. Britain rather than her homeland became her focus when judging the United States. This allowed her to acknowledge America's problems before she immigrated and erased the need for a narrative of seductiveness to explain the decision to move. Elizabeth's recollections revolved around the issues of race, crime, and economic opportunity: "As a black person, you don't really stand a chance, a very rich country, but full of crime."

Elizabeth's decision to immigrate stemmed from a chance encounter in 1979 while visiting her parents, who were living in California. It related to her husband: "While we were here, my husband then at the time ran into one of his schoolteachers from England, who offered him a job here. We were on the streets in San Francisco." The job came with the possibility of significant improvement in her socioeconomic status: "And then when we had the job offer, we had to go back to England, and I'd been here for a month. So when we went back to England, I suddenly saw the major difference in the economy and how much more ahead we could be if we lived here." In other words, America represented an escape from the social and economic limitations of Great Britain.

Because she compared her opportunities for improvement with those in Great Britain, Elizabeth was able to claim the loss of economic and social status that she enjoyed at home and not compromise it by acknowledging the material benefits of immigration. She was comfortable describing the opportunities for affluence in her country of origin that were foreclosed by immigration: "If I lived in my country, like my friends do, I would have my maid and my cook. You know that lifestyle? Here, I live well. And it probably—it would appear if I was at home that I would have a more affluent lifestyle."

Elizabeth offered personal explanations for her decision to remain in the United States, presenting immigration as an escape from the strictures of family and an opportunity to win individual freedom:

> When I leave there and come back here, I'm glad I'm back here because, you know, I feel a lot more comfortable. My home is here, and I'm older. The benefits that I want. . . . At home, I'm always a child. I'm always looked at—what my family was. I'm always judged by who my family is. Here, I'm an individual. People only see me for who I am. And that's all they know about me, and that's all, you know, I put forth, but once I go back home, then they'll—I don't feel an individual when I go back there. I am one of a family. Here I am on my own.

But Elizabeth's desire for escape was full of contradiction and ambiguity. She expressed a strong need for constant "reconnection" with her country of origin, which she satisfied by visiting at least once every two years. She said she had made more than fifteen of these visits between 1979 and 1994, when the interview was conducted. She had also bought property in her homeland that she needed to "check out" periodically.

Despite refusing to identify herself specifically as West Indian, Elizabeth considers the Caribbean to be her home. She speaks of her presence in the United States in terms of drawbacks and sacrifices represented by images of loss, freedom, family, and friendships. These she considered to be the essence of her being and more significant in defining her humanity than the benefits of being a U.S. resident:

> I don't have the—the big thing that I missed is that I don't have the freedom to just take off, you know, on a nine-to-five job, an eight-to-four job, I could stop at the end of my day, and go to the beach, swim when I come home. I don't have the freedom of just going out and at family gatherings, having all my family with me, everybody. Instead it's me and my small group, but not all my extended family. I still think that because of the distances, we've gotten so blasé that we don't keep in the same contact. The contacts are not close. The friendships are not close because everybody's running off to do their own thing. I think that we're driven by money. I came for the economics, and I said that was the good part,

but we've become driven by it where we give up everything for it. Whereas when I go back to the Caribbean, I go back to the simple life, and maybe this life has made me more aware of that one, and made it more affordable to me, but you know, there's a big contrast.

Elizabeth speaks of her life in the United States almost in terms of a loss of community:

> I have had to give up my freedom. I find I've become more protective of my personal life in a way as far as I don't just meet you and tell you everything about me. This is different, but you don't get that out of me. You'd have to meet me a few times before I could trust you. The trust is not as far because I don't really know who you are. On the islands, I know you. I've seen you probably in six or seven places in one day, I automatically know who you are. So the trust is much less here.

Her commitment to the United States seems almost functional. She explains her decision to become a citizen in terms of the benefits it provides: "I thought if I was going to live in the country that I wanted all the benefits of that country." California has given Elizabeth an opportunity to realize her foreign essence while living in the United States. She sees the state as existing in the interstice between her country and America, an idea she presents by referring to the state's physical geography and the possibility of realizing some of the privileges of light complexion that she had enjoyed in her homeland. The accommodation of her foreignness is demonstrated by its acceptance by California's residents. In addition, Elizabeth's accent takes on a special significance in her identific self-representation. At the same time, however, she recognizes California as part of the United States, particularly in its racialized discourse of difference:

> How my impressions have changed, what I also initially kind of felt once I was here was that people were very friendly in California and very considerate, and color didn't really seem to matter. What my impression changed over the years was that was in fact not true. And that, you know, because I had an accent or whatever, and my color was lighter that I was acceptable in certain areas, but when it really got down to it, that there still is very much a racial problem.

Elizabeth's foreignness became the basis for her acceptance in California on her own terms and provided an escape from American blackness. White Americans were prepared to accept and acknowledge the superiority that was integral to her self-understanding and derived from her class and color, even if such acceptance was only in comparison with African Americans:

> Well, for example, I have some European friends, and we had a discussion about, you know, the African American, and I remember one—a couple of them commenting to me, "Well, you're not the same. You can't class yourself and them because you're different. Your color is different. Your accent is different. You don't"—they saw the African American in a derogatory light that put me a little above them, and therefore to them, that was acceptable.

> I just see myself as a person with you know whatever qualities I come with. I don't put myself in a category. I don't ever limit myself. I just know that I am me. I don't put myself in a box, you know. I don't put any limits on myself.

While Elizabeth acknowledged the significance of race, she located herself above it, which allowed her to cope with it while denying its personal consequences. She spoke of herself almost as a sympathetic and engaged spectator:

> I haven't really run into any problems. My husband now is American, African American, and I haven't run into any problems with it. But I know from time to time, I would hear like a comedian, or like if I watch a television show, I would see that they think of us very differently. But I personally haven't experienced anything.

Implicit here is the notion that her engagement with American racism derives from her marriage to an African American. This seems to justify her racial concerns despite her sense of difference from American blackness. It also permits her to acknowledge America's racial problems and the need for redress.

The dilemma for West Indians in their self-conceptualizations as permanent foreigners is that they are forced to confront the racial realities of the United States while constructing narratives of difference. In recounting their experiences, they acknowledge the discriminatory and stereotypical consequences of America's racism. At the same time, in their self-representations as "special," West Indians in the Bay Area believe that once their uniqueness is acknowledged, they will escape racial categorization. This, to them, explains their history as racial pioneers. Elizabeth presents herself as having made this racial breakthrough in her occupation, although she recognizes that the sociopolitical climate of civil rights made her success possible. As a West Indian, her success was preordained; without affirmative action, it would merely have been more difficult to achieve:

> Affirmative action. I think that has helped. I think it's helped here, and I think it's helped—even though it can be a negative thing, it's helped me to get into some positions when I initially came here, but had no choice. You know, I was the only one of two people of color working in the position I was in, and the other girl was Jamaican, and they had to have us there. You know, we were good, but they didn't realize that until after, but because of affirmative action, they had to have us. Everybody else that was of color was a maid, was in housekeeping. You know, they just kept the numbers there so they didn't—they didn't give you the opportunity. I think I would have had to fight more for it. Once I got it, I moved up quickly, but initially, I don't think I would have had that opportunity. So I think through affirmative action, I was able to move very quickly through the system, through—also through my education. I think, you know, coming as a foreigner, I was coming with a lot more. They weren't ready for some of the things that I was throwing out to them.

Like the other West Indian respondents, Elizabeth considers family and a sense of social responsibility and security as lacking in the United States. These are distinguishing features of West Indians and, indeed, of other "Third World" immigrant communities:

> In the Caribbean, even though, you know, after seventeen years old, I got home, if my parents weren't there, there was a maid at home, or there was somebody at the house ready to meet us, or grandparents. Now I think now with more Asian, with more cultures coming in, Third World countries, too, I think I'm seeing more where parents, grandparents are living together. So kids are now beginning to get extended families. But it's lonely for kids coming home, the American kids. They just come home to nothing. Like I always came home to something. When we grew up, I never had—I never had a key to my front door. I never had a key to any door. I never did. Now I lock everything even to walk two minutes from my car, I lock up.

Elizabeth believes that her West Indian identity is maintained through connections with her homeland and family. The social network of West Indians in the Bay Area plays little, if any, role in her social construction of self. It provides her only with the opportunity to participate in cultural renewal. She does not recognize the existence of a West Indian community in the Bay Area, but she acknowledges the importance of connections to West Indians and to participation in their cultural events: "I would say I—you know, there isn't a community as such, but you know, when they get in touch with me and let me know something's going on, I'm there." So she feels free to have a very diverse group of friends: "I've got West Indian friends. I've got African American friends. I've got white friends."

Elizabeth's residence in California has contributed significantly to the social construction of her identity as a permanent foreigner. While the state is part of the United States, it also exists on its margins, allowing her to be a West Indian and to live a life as if she were in her homeland. She retains strong physical connections to "home" that are objectified in visits and in the ownership of property. Her West Indianness comes with some of the privileges of class and color that are part her sense of self and that she would have if she were living at home. At the same time, however, she accommodates her blackness through her African American husband, which explains and justifies her concern with race. Elizabeth is willing to acknowledge the role of race in limiting her opportunities for equality, but she sees these limitations as merely temporary. That is, they are removed when her foreignness is acknowledged, with her accent an important signifier of her foreign status.

Richard Brandon

Permanent immigrants might construct self-understandings as cosmopolitan subjects. While their identities derive from their countries of origin, they occupy an urban space by means of their cultural capital of acquired skills, education, tastes, and styles. They have outgrown their countries of origin because of their urbanity. But their social identities are firmly planted in their country of origin, which becomes the basis of their uniqueness.

Richard Brandon grew up "struggling somewhat" in his homeland but left his country of birth to attend university, first in the West Indies and then in Great Britain. He is at pains to point out that his bachelor's degree, which he received in a science subject from the University College of the West Indies, was actually a "University of London degree." The latter, he explains, was the university that "was giving out the exams and the degrees." So he describes his university education as being "joint between the University of the West Indies and the University of London." Richard subsequently went to graduate school in the West Indies, after which he moved to Great Britain and worked in a technical field while attending graduate school. Richard speaks of his time in Great Britain as critical to the development of his technical skills:

I had always revered British institutions in my area of expertise for their objectivity, for their high quality. And I was interested to see how they operated, and how they did it. And I got a chance to see how they did it, and to be part of it. And so a lot of those things helped me. It's part of the training that helped me and helps me to get the total picture related to my current work. So yes, that was always instrumental in honing and sharpening my skills.

Because of the difficulty of working and studying at the same time, Richard decided to come to the United States, where he attended graduate school at one of the Bay Area's prestigious universities. He earned an M.A. and a Ph.D. Richard emphasized that he decided on his field of expertise with reference to the needs of the West Indies. He "elected" to become qualified "in an area that would be a benefit to the Caribbean." In this way, he was able to separate the technical superiority of the United States from the human qualities making up his own essence.

Richard's identity is very much tied to his role as a modernizer, one that cannot be realized in the United States. During the periods between universities, Richard worked in several senior and influential positions in both his home country and the Caribbean region. He became well known in the area for his contribution to its development. His role as the bearer of modernity to the Caribbean derived from his ability to earn graduate degrees and from the ideas of the industrial North:

My experience in my home country is one of growing up, maturing, and then doing service for my country, and being able to help folks, to motivate them, be able to bring them to an appreciation of the finer things. So that my experience was more helping our country growing and maturing and participating in it.

Richard described some of the modern innovations that he brought to the Caribbean, including one that introduced satellite technology.

At the same time, Richard sees himself as having a "nostalgic" connection to his homeland. His experiences when growing up and maturing there have shaped his sense of being, as has his leadership role in the Caribbean. He thus has a uniqueness not available to African Americans:

West Indians, if they're treated differently, it's not surprising because they are different. We have come through so many different experiences where we're able to sift through what are the best reactions for different situations. So people treat us, might treat us differently because of that—because we have taken the situation and reacted differently. In the case of politics, very often, you hear West Indians talk with great pride about nationalism and what they're doing and what they're not doing, and the same thing cannot be true for our Latinos and Asians and some black Americans because they're not from an island culture. They cannot say that with that degree of panache, that degree of aplomb, that degree of real strong, rooted confidence. And so someone in listening to the various groups would say, "Well, these West Indians seem know what they're about. They seem to be very self-confident and the like." The next thing is that West Indians know they come here for something. Black Americans, this is their country. They expect more, more than we do, and rightly so. It's their country, and they should expect more than we do. But we came here looking for something. When we get at something, we try to do more. So we very often were not involved in a lot of the black struggles. Not from our everyday lives, emanating from our everyday life. It's more from solidarity, it's more from support that we find ourselves involved in it. Not from fighting for my right in my own homeland. And so that helps to structure our interactions, and we fought that, and so therefore we're likely to be treated different.

Richard's modernity and cosmopolitanism, defined by his technical and managerial skills, set him apart from the rest of society. He can do his work anywhere in the world. His presence in the United States is explained as a consequence of natural disaster in his homeland. With his return impractical, Richard merely transferred to the United States his plans for establishing a research and management organization in the Caribbean. He eventually became vice-president of operations and head of administration at a research and management institution in the Bay Area. As a result, he is able to live without the sense of responsibility and commitment that defines his self-identity as West Indian.

Even though Richard can live anywhere in the world, he belongs to his homeland. He describes himself as a West Indian who lives in the United States. His country of origin is his "first home," to which he feels a sense of obligation, and the United States is his "second home," which he treats with objective detachment. This explains his ability to analyze his country of residence and to admit prior knowledge of its problems before he decided to immigrate:

From the point of view of if there is any one dominant macro impression, it's that it was a very large land of splendid opportunity, but huge problems, racial problems, equity problems, and being a superpower, world problems. So that's sort of the general impression that I had, that it's not an easy place to go.

Richard's sees himself as occupying a metropolitan space in the United States occupied by other cosmopolitans. He has little need to join the West Indian community. His origins and his role as modernizer combine to shape an identity that needs little renewal in the community's participatory rituals. Instead, he is free to participate in a diverse social circle without jeopardizing his identity as a West Indian. His social circle is made up of

people whom I've met at work, and people who I've met close to where I live. People I've met through social events that we get to know. Non-Caribbean people that I have met at conferences or at university and have retained a very high degree of closeness with them. Many of them just Americans, others are Europeans.

Richard feels a special obligation to other West Indians but does not see himself as connected to the West Indian community.

The key thing is not to meeting all the time. The key thing is being around and knowing that somebody's there so that if they need you to help them with a problem, help them to adjust, or help them with something that they know where to go and where you are. So that is the only thing that is on my mind in terms of how I retain my association with the Caribbean community in this area.

Richard's sense of cosmopolitanism does not demand physical connection with his homeland. He rarely returns to the Caribbean, even though he "would go back to live there anytime," but only "to retire with the freedom to go anywhere, live in the Caribbean for part of the time and live in the United States or elsewhere for another part of the time." But he admits that he misses his home and his people and that he had to give up a lot when he decided to immigrate: "When immigrating, you have to make those choices and live within those choices. So I think some of the drawbacks have to do with the fact that some of the things I love the most are not in America." Nonetheless, he has returned only twice to his island of origin since immigrating fourteen years before the interview. Both instances were to attend family-related ceremonies.

Richard's cosmopolitanism leads to a sense of living in two worlds. The first is the modern environment of the skilled and educated elite, who have no sense of difference and who are judged by their skill and capacities. The second is the ordinary world of day-to-day existence. One cannot escape the rules of existence in this ordinary world and its terms of organization. Richard was forced to enter the day-to-day world of the United States only after obtaining his Ph.D., and he was prepared to accept its terms of participation:

> I arrived in a university setting. So to some extent, it was a little bit sheltered from reality of what goes on because you arrive at a university, which gives you an umbrella, and you are able to get housing for you and your family. You get relatively cheap housing, but good housing. You get good, good food because the university is situated in a very good town, which has excellent public schools and the like. So while studying, one is somewhat isolated from the harsh reality of the society. My impressions remained quite positive and quite strong while I was a student. When I stopped being a student, a lot of the edges started to sharpen. And some of the bad started to hit, and some of the more difficult aspects of this society like racism and the difficulty of opportunity if you're not part of the dominant culture raised its troublesome head with me, and I just had to overcome that. You have to remember always that you're not in your own home and that we choose to come to the United States. You have to adjust.

Richard also was willing to adjust to America's racial discrimination, which he accepts. He does not need to claim a special, nonracialized status because of his West Indianness. His "specialness" comes from his role in the scientific community. So although Richard recognizes the effects of U.S. racism, he is at pains to deny its role in judgments of his professional and scientific competence:

> I experience racial discrimination all the time. From the day I stepped here, I've been discriminated [against] all the time. I choose to turn my back—I turn my back on it. I don't want to make an issue out of it. I see people who greet me at some point, and other times when I'm walking by, they look down at their shoes so they won't have to look at me in the face. I have experienced it in the workplace, and I don't want to—because this is a topic I don't want to get involved into reviewing bad stuff. I've experienced it all and everywhere you go. Everywhere you go, whether I had to be a consultant. I hear people give me excellent praise because I articulate very well. I have a very nice accent. I speak very well when I give speeches, and stuff like that. But they act surprised that I can

do that. It's not that it's not a good compliment. It's just the way in which it's said. All of that's some form of racism in my opinion. But I don't react to that.

Richard's sense of permanent foreignness is underscored by his decision not to become a U.S. citizen, a decision related to his strong sense of belonging to his country of origin and the absence of a sense of obligation to the United States:

> I don't know if I ever will want to become a citizen of the United States. I may decide to do it. Right now, it hasn't got any strong, strong appeal to me, Apart from voting. I don't think about that privilege. I'm one of the strong people who like my country.

Richard's sense of permanent foreignness also refers to a cosmopolitanism that cannot be accommodated in his country of origin. So he has been forced to seek a wider universe after fulfilling his obligation to bring modernity to his homeland and the West Indies as a whole. His uniqueness in the universe is related to his participatory experiences in his homeland and the West Indies and also to the skills and qualifications that he acquired in Britain and the United States. His cosmopolitan identity allows him to deal with the real world, whether the limitations of his home or the problems he faces as a black man in America. The former are "his" problems with which national obligations demand engagement, and the latter are the consequences of not belonging, which have to be endured because of his foreignness. Despite having to face discrimination "all the time," Richard believes that he has to "turn my back on it. I don't want to make an issue of it. It's their problem not mine. I just let it go."

Permanent Foreigners: Notions of Home

For permanent foreigners, America is not, and can never be, home. There are practical reasons for living in the United States that may force them to spend the rest of their lives in the country. For many West Indian immigrants, the decision to come to the United States was not theirs. Most of the forty-five respondents immigrated in order to join family. Those who did not came to get a higher education. Only one came to the United States for reasons other than these.

Economic opportunity and the establishment of a family explain the

West Indians' continued presence in the United States. They all expected to return, regardless of how long they had been in the United States and despite the possibility that they could not return because of continued political and economic crises. This was true, for example, for the respondents from Guyana:

> I'll always consider Guyana my home, but because I've been here for over twenty-five years, I guess, you think of it as home, but you think of—you're still going to go back home, eventually you're going to go back home to the West Indies. I think I would rather go live in St. Lucia or Grenada, at this point. Maybe because I haven't been back in such a long time. I'm not sure. I would go back to West Indies, but I'm not sure if I want to go to Guyana.

Even those who considered California home expected to return. They always had a pragmatic reason for staying in California, but it did not compensate for their sense of foreignness and difference:

> My immediate family is here. Most of my relatives are in the United States, but for me personally, right now, home is in California. Well, even though I consider California home, I think it's for the benefit of my kids. I think I would like them to basically get involved with—actually I would prefer to have them grow up where I came from, to be honest with you, for the schooling because I think it would just make them think better for them. I think they would have a different view in terms of what life is all about, and I think their focus would be different.

For this respondent, family and an American wife meant that he could not return, despite the considerable drawbacks to remaining in the United States, pertaining primarily to his American-born children:

> Yeah, my wife is an American, so that would make it difficult. First of all, my wife would have to like being in my country before I even considered basically taking the kids back there. They grew up in America. So like that, it would be—I guess my job would be pretty difficult in terms of—when I try to instill my values in terms of the way I grew up. But still I think the bottom line is the environment in which—that surrounds them, it makes it much more difficult. You try to instill your values, and you try to do as best as you can with the kids, but it does help if the surrounding environment basically is the same in terms of what you're trying to instill in your kids.

As foreigners, West Indians in Northern California believe that they came with cultural values lacking in the United States. These are the bases of both their difference and their superiority. West Indians use narratives and memories of home to judge the moral and ethical deficiencies of their host country. On the one hand, they see themselves as the embodiment of the morality and ethics that are absent in the United States. But on the other hand, they fear the polluting effects of exposure to the American way. Accordingly, they use their self-representations of difference and foreignness to resist being absorbed into America's ethical and moral morass. This makes it impossible for West Indians in the San Francisco Bay to become transformed into Americans.

The West Indian identity emerges out of family, community, discipline, respect, security, obedience, freedom, predictability, simplicity and happiness, which set West Indians apart from "Americans." They are what makes it important for them to recount their experiences before their immigration:

> Memory, memories. The kind of freedom to move around, do things in a more cooperative spirit and share with your neighbors without asking any questions. Here is the difference. You could probably ask your neighbor for some rice here, but you wouldn't get it. But at home if you ask your neighbor for some rice, you're going to get your rice. The culture, it was a kind of community. We are just all over ourselves in America.

> We were a very close knit family, extended family. Houses tended to be close together and everyone is related to each other. So you never have to worry about a babysitter or anything like that. And just very, very close knit family. And that is what I remember from living in the Caribbean.

> Beautiful, really beautiful. Not very stressful, and everyday you wake up, you know exactly what you had to do, and you could actually set your pace without over extending yourself, and there was quite a lot of time for relaxation and pleasure, both with the family and as an individual.

> When I first came here I was troubled. I'd have this recurring dream I'm running in my schoolyard as a kid in my elementary school which is tranquillity. That's when I was free, and everything was like you don't even think about tomorrow.

> What I remember most from growing up at home is that like I tell my kids, they haven't gotten the opportunity to experience the goodness of growing up in the islands as a child. At the bottom of my village where we lived, we had like a small little park, and all the kids used to gather there and play.

> It was more like a village where everybody was your parent. Everybody in the village was your parent. You go to school, and the teachers, of course,

had more control over you than they have here. You do something wrong on the streets, you wouldn't have to wait until you get home to be scolded. Whoever saw you doing wrong had the authority to scold you.

You are living. Because here you are just existing. Its just from day to day. But there, there's so much you can do and see and experience.

A sense of accomplishment, achievement, and success is integral to the self-representations of West Indians in the San Francisco Bay Area. Most acknowledged the opportunities made available by immigrating, and almost all of them saw their achievement in the United States as made inevitable by their background. Achievement and success were merely logical continuations of their conditions at home. In the United States, success comes with a loss of morality and ethics.

Thus, all but four of the respondents claimed either a middle-class or comfortable background not lacking in material necessities. In this regard, West Indians reject popular understandings of American opportunity. In recounting their backgrounds, they described a homeland that had a more humane social culture. The respondents used their claims to middle-class status to reject the superiority of American materialism and the American view of their countries as impoverished. Narratives about sufficiency at home became indictments of American values and were used as to diminish the benefits of immigrating. For example, West Indians were acutely aware of the existence of hunger and homelessness in the United States, and these became important indices of their own superiority:

I would say upper middle class because I had, I grew up knowing nothing about hunger, about being hungry. I know they had poor people, yes, but it is a different poor to here. You see? Because what we would call poor there is not that people don't live in houses. They have homes, but it is just that they might not have enough money to get what they want, or something like that.

We never was hungry. We'd grow our own things and chicken and stuff.

Many used their backgrounds to contest American claims to the "good life," downplaying the importance of money and possessions in favor of alternative values of name, home life, contentment, happiness, and knowledge:

Life was good. Really good, because we had a kind of royalty life back home. Just carrying on the name. Our name said a lot.

Life was very easy. Everybody enjoyed it. I guess everybody had a good life. We enjoyed living at home.

The way I was raised, even though I didn't want for anything materially, my parents always made sure that I knew the value of what I had. So I think that was very, very good on their part to have done that.

I guess, what would you call it? Middle income? We didn't have too much money really. But I was happy. I had a happy childhood. I was satisfied with what I had. I think I have too much now.

I would say my parents are both fairly well educated. My father was very highly read. So we were considered middle class. We were not poor. We had property. We lived on my grandmother's farm, so we had property. We were not poverty stricken, no. But we didn't own a car. Compared to standards in America, we did not own a car and so forth.

Identity, Education, and Achievement

Education is critical to the self-representations of West Indians in the San Francisco Bay Area. Many acknowledged that residence in the United States came with opportunities for higher education not available in their countries of origin. But mere access was not enough to explain West Indians' achievement. Rather, their success was in the foundation of discipline, application, and fundamentals laid in their country of origin. As Americans, particularly as black Americans, this achievement and success would have been impossible. Thus their achievements derived not from America but from their qualities as West Indians:

> You couldn't compare a high-school graduate from the Caribbean to a high-school graduate in the United States. I mean, we would tear them apart in terms of a classical educational background.

> Up to high-school level in Jamaica, I would say is much better, better as in more advanced. And then, college level is probably better or about the same.

> In the United States, I don't think education was created for the people as such. Education was created for a particular group of people, or an even higher education is a privilege for some, and not a right when it should be a right. Those who can seize the opportunity and take advantage of it, do so. But if you are being left behind, I don't think that one is really concerned about that. And that has to do with the overall structuring

and the nature of society. It is not important. Education is not important. It is not a primary focus of this society. It is only a focus for those who feel that they have to be in control.

Well, for one, teachers are not allowed to flog kids here, and I think some of the kids here need to be disciplined. If they were disciplined, they wouldn't have all of these problems with guns and drugs ensuing in the schools. See, I think so. There's also the issue of uniforms. All of the schools in Grenada have uniforms.

I have a high respect for the educational system here, but I really have a lot of respect for the educational system back home. That's because, I think here . . . back home, if you are doing something, you know why you do it. Here, you know what you have to do, but you don't have the real foundation as to why you are doing it. I don't think the kids have the solid foundation as to what they are doing, and why they are doing it. I think if they know why they are doing certain things, they'll do it.

Believe it or not, the system in Jamaica is much better. Is much higher. However, this is a problem. And this is a fundamental issue. In terms of the school system, high-school system. Its much higher because it's much more demanding. But the downside is if you don't do well, there aren't ways of getting back into it. And this is really the advantage of the American system.

I think our foundation education in the Caribbean is much stronger than America's foundation. Elementary, secondary—which is what you call high school. I think that education is much stronger, much wider. And this has helped me a lot in my life.

A young child growing up and seeking education, I think and I know that education in the West Indies is superior to the education here. The background, the grammar. But once you finish with high school, I would recommend college here for my children.

Within the Caribbean, there's much more structure. And like that, the many distractions were not there. I guess I am a firm believer that if you give people too much room to do what they want to do within any type of system, then I think it has a negative impact on the overall, on the average student.

If I ever had children, I wouldn't want them to go to public school here because I think it's really sad. I don't understand how children can go to school, graduate from school, and not be able to read, or not be able to write, have any kind of command over the English language. That really disturbs me. In the Caribbean, everybody gets to go to school. You don't get kicked out because you are poor. Here, you don't have to pay for books. You don't have to pay for school. And I really don't know why especially minorities don't receive a good education here. I don't know why that's the case. I mean, I went to school in a Third World country, but I got a better education than I could get in a First World country in America. I think teachers in the Caribbean take a personal interest in their students.

I just remember the schooling being very different in what was expected. And my fundamentals, whatever fundamentals I have now came from there.

Access and resources are the defining features of the educational system in the United States and differentiate it from education in the home country. The United States provides opportunities where none would exist at home. At the same time, West Indians are critical of the way that educational resources are used in this country. While resources and access make a difference for them, they do not deliver a sound education to many other Americans with different backgrounds. Sometimes, even the absence of resources can be beneficial:

Here in America, there is a lot of resources. There is a lot of help. There is a lot of libraries. There is a lot of educational aids. In the West Indies you don't have all that. In the West Indies, when you had to do math, you had to start a problem from the beginning to the end and you had to do it by hand. In the West Indies, you can tell how you arrived at your answers. Here, you can use a calculator. There is all kinds of aids in school. You don't have to tell the teacher how the problem, what steps you took to get to that answer. Here there are so much aids that the kids don't know how to tell you how they arrived at certain situations.

It's accessible to everyone who wants it. If somebody wants an education in America, it doesn't matter how poor you are or how rich you are. I think once you're determined, it is there for you.

There's probably more opportunities in that the fundamentals are very good in the Caribbean. But maybe the computer and technology and resources may not be.

America has a very good educational system. I don't think people get it the way they should. The system just seems to not work for a lot of people. I mean, if you look at the amount of people who can't read and write the way they should. I don't know.

They have it made here, and so they take everything for granted because the fact is that everything in this country, everything is much more sophisticated. Here every kid has a calculator, but there a calculator is a luxury. And so because you don't have a calculator, or maybe because your parents couldn't afford it, you knew you had to learn to multiply, or had to divide in order to make it to the next grade. You see, so, at an early age we knew the importance of learning certain things, of reading.

Despite the resources and access, West Indians' success is invariably tied to the foundation of learning laid at home:

When I came over here, I was ahead. They put me back according to my age, although I was ahead of the other students. Schools in the Caribbean, they tend to be a little bit more advanced than here, so what you are learning in high school, they are already learning in grammar school. Especially when it comes to math and things, math and the sciences.

You go to the islands, the education is good. You go to the secondary school, it's almost to the level of the colleges here. You finish primary school on any one of the islands, its almost like a high-school level here.

Conclusion

The social identities of permanent foreigners are shaped by participatory experiences and images of home. These are cognitive constructs that respond to the immigrants' understanding of their own social position in the social geography and also to nationalist notions of belonging in their host environment. These notions are counteracted by their own sense of identity. Their sense of superiority explains permanent foreigners' inability to be mixed into the "melting pot" of national identity in their country of residence. Rather, they see themselves as bearers of qualities and values lacking in their host country, and they assign the benefits of immigrating to the practicalities of life. This view says nothing about fundamental values that are threatened by immigration and can be absorbed by the host society. West Indians' status as permanent foreigners protects against this loss.

Permanent foreigners shape their identities in accordance with their own participatory experiences in both their home and host country. Their sense of foreignness is shaped by their interpretations of these experiences. West Indians in the San Francisco Bay Area separate themselves from the rest of America to avoid the implications of racism and to mitigate its consequences. They see themselves as "special" because of their achievements, which they attribute to values of their homeland that made their success inevitable. If they were Americans, such achievement would be impossible. As West Indians, it is inevitable.

The identities of permanent foreigners are crystallized around myths of eventual return shared by members of the West Indian community in Northern California. They reinforce their sense of belonging to their country of origin, even for those who define California as home or who acknowledge that social, political, and economic conditions may make their return impractical. When West Indians do acknowledge their connections to the United States, they usually attribute them to marriage to Americans and to their American-born children. In sum, their identity as permanent foreigners allows West Indians in the Bay Area to manage the contradictions between their blackness and their achievement.

Epilogue
The Construction of Identity

In the United States, notions of race are the reference schemata of identity and are at the center of the cognitive constructs that inform identity. It is through such notions that meaning is assigned to social difference.

Although race determines the broad categories of identity, it is complicated and modified by a number of factors. Racially defined subjects bring their cultural baggage to arenas of social interaction, which support self-understandings that may differ from popular conceptualizations of "who they are." Racial idioms also are modified and reformulated in the geosocial environment, differentiating the meanings ascribed to racialized subjects across different geographic and social arenas. Identity is complicated by another factor as well. Individuals have available to them alternative notions of belonging that they can choose when constructing their self-identities. These may conflict with racialized constructs of difference.

In the United States, a person's identity is a combination of individual, social, cultural, and spatial differences in racialized meaning. It is complicated by the choices made available from the myriad of alternative definitions of self. Individual self-definitions take their cues from the collective identities formed from the particularities of highly localized geosocial arenas and are combined with the person's own history and participatory experiences to form the basis for identity negotiation.

West Indian identity in the San Francisco Bay Area is a confrontation with and negotiation of the racialized atmosphere of the United States. At the most basic level, West Indians are forced to define themselves, both collectively and individually, in relation to the African American community to which they are racially bound. The choices of identity available to them are circumscribed by their social and geographic location in the political economy of Northern California. Northern California provides abundant opportunities for skilled and educated people but almost no opportunities for the unskilled and uneducated. This has produced a West Indian immigrant community whose members generally have a high socioeconomic status. In their self-representations, West Indians publicize their high status in rituals and performances aimed at incorporating notions of success and achievement in popular understandings of who they are. Success and achievement are expected of members of the West Indian community. Those lacking the social and economic capital of the middle and professional classes are marginalized, isolated, and excluded from the displays and performances of West Indian identity.

West Indians use popular stereotypical images to locate themselves outside American understandings of racial difference. They do this through symbolic displays that confirm and reinforce their exotic foreignness in American popular imagination. Through these displays, West Indian immigrants in the San Francisco Bay Area establish themselves in the group of permanent foreigners identified with California's technological and financial success.

Success, achievement, and permanent foreignness also separate West Indians from African Americans in the public consciousness. In this sense, the social construction of West Indian identity in the San Francisco Bay Area is the product of negotiated responses to American discourses of racial difference. By being "not American," West Indians exclude themselves from collective understandings of blackness and from American racial types.

At the same time, West Indians depend on the social and political power of the African American community for access to opportunity, for professional and occupational support, and for protection from discrimination and prejudice. So although they assert their blackness when constructing their identity, they use narratives of personal and collective histories that differ significantly from the black experience in the United States. West Indians highlight social and cultural agency and political and economic self-determination in the constructed memories of their homeland. These memories support claims of superior morality and meritorious achievement. Experiences of oppression and of white domination are presented in these narratives of difference to explain African American immorality and underachievement. West Indians' experiences of their homeland enable them to overcome the limitations of race in the United States.

Recognition of their differences enables West Indians in the San Francisco Bay Area to look objectively at American racism and its consequences. Although they acknowledge the presence of racism and its potential effects on their lives and opportunities, they see it as a problem that can be circumvented, negotiated, or ignored. And they use their personal experiences as confirmation.

Some West Indians develop relational and emotional connections with African Americans. A few in the study did so because they identified as blacks. Others were forced into the racial schisms of American society. Enlistment in the military produced one set of conditions for insertion into American society. Social isolation from West Indian communities produced another. But the particularities of West Indian identity construction in the San Francisco Bay Area impose conditions on West Indians' relationships with African Americans, making such relationships tentative and highly selective and, often, untenable. For such relationships to be maintained, African American partners may be forced into accommodations and identific compromises. The absence of bridging mechanisms and a history of mutual understanding makes switching identities difficult. As a result, West Indians rarely become involved in these relationships as African Americans. This is true even for those who have been excluded and isolated from the identific practices of the West Indian community. Rather, their African American partners and friends are forced to adapt, sometimes becoming West Indians in the process.

West Indians' identity limits their association with African Americans to the middle and professional classes. By confining their associations to successful African Americans, West Indians protect their identity from being discredited in their claims to morality, success, and achievement. At the same time, such associations ensure West Indians of access to the social, political, and occupational networks of the African American middle and professional classes.

In their current social construction, West Indians in Northern California can never become Americans, for to do so would be to accept an African American identity. Unlike the West Indians in New York, they have no ethnicized options available to them as alternative identities. Like the African American educated and professional classes, they seek escape from the stereotypical images of American blackness, and they use their status as immigrants to differentiate their claims of belonging to their country of residence and also to their country of origin. In the social and cultural context of California, they are able to make legitimate claims of belonging to both.

References

Allen, S. 1971. New Minorities and old Conflicts. New York: Random House

Allen-Taylor, Douglas. 1998. "Carnaval Atmosphere." San Jose, Calif.: San Jose State University, Department of Continuing Education, Metro-Active Features, September 9. [Internet webpage]

Baker, Jean H. 1983. Affairs of Party: The Political Culture of Northern Democrats in the Mid-Nineteenth Century. Ithaca, N.Y. : Cornell University Press.

Bell, David A. 1985. "The Triumph of Asian-Americans." The New Republic, July 15–22, pp. 24–31.

Blackwell, J. E. 1991. The Black Community: Diversity and Unity. New York: HarperCollins.

Bogen, E. 1988. "Caribbean Immigrants in New York City: A Demographic Summary." New York: New York City Department of Planning.

Bryce-Laporte, R. S. 1973. "New York City and the New Caribbean Immigration: A Contextual Statement." International Migration Review 13, no 2: 214–34.

Bryce-Laporte, R. S., and D. Mortimer, eds. 1976. "Caribbean Immigration in the United States." Research Institute on Immigration and Ethnic Studies, Occasional Papers no. 1. Washington, D.C. : Smithsonian Institution.

Bunch, Lonnie G. 1990. "A Past Not Necessarily Prologue: The Afro-American in Los Angeles." In 20th Century Los Angeles, ed. Norman M. Klein and Martin J. Schiesl. Claremont, Calif.: Regina Books.

Butcher, Kristin F. 1994. "Black Immigrants in the United States: A Comparison with Native Blacks and Other Immigrants." Industrial and Labor Relations Review 47: 265–85.

California Association of Realtors. 2000. "Home Sales, Median Home Price Hit All-Time Highs in March." News release. April 25. [Internet homepage]

California Department of Finance, Demographic Research Unit. 1999. "Population and Percent Distribution by Race and Hispanic Origin" (Table B-5).

California Statistical Abstract. July 1997. [Internet webpage]

Colen, S. 1989. "Just a Little Respect: West Indian Domestic Workers in New York City." In Muchachas No More: Household Workers in Latin American and the Caribbean, ed. E. Chaney and M. G. Castro, pp. 171–96. Philadelphia: Temple University Press.

Davison, R. B. 1962. *West Indian Migrants: Social and Economic Facts of Migration from the West Indies*. New York: Oxford University Press.

De Vos, George. 1973. *Socialization for Achievement: Essays on the Cultural Psychology of the Japanese*. Berkeley and Los Angeles: University of California Press.

DeWitt, K. 1990. "Immigrants Look Outside New York for a Better Life." *New York Times*, September 4, p. B3.

Dodoo, F. Nil-Amoo. 1991. "Earnings Differences among Blacks in America." *Social Science Research* 20: 93–108.

Dymally, Mervyn M. 1972. "The Rise of Black Political Leadership in California." In *What Black Politicians Are Saying*, ed. Nathan Wright Jr., pp. 32–43. New York: Hawthorn Books.

Fan, M., M. Finnegan, and J. Siegel. 1997. "Cheers and Jeers Greet the Mayor." *New York Daily News*, September 2, p. 17.

Farley, Reynolds, and Walter Allen. 1987. *The Color Line and the Quality of Life in America*. New York: Russell Sage Foundation.

Fisher, Sethard. 1992. *From Margin to Mainstream: The Social Progress of Black Americans*. 2d ed. Lanham, Md.: Rowman & Littlefield.

Foner, N. 1978. *Jamaica Farewell: Jamaican Migrants in London*. Berkeley and Los Angeles: University of California Press.

———, ed. 1987. *New Immigrants in New York*. New York: Columbia University Press.

Fong, Coleen V. 1989. "Tracing the Origins of a 'Model Minority.' A Study of the Depictions of Chinese Americans in Popular Magazines." Ph.D. diss., University of Oregon.

Gilroy, P. 1993. *The Black Atlantic: Modernity and Double Consciousness*. London: Verso.

———. 1997. "Between Camps: Race and Culture in Postmodernity." Professorial inaugural lecture. University of London, Goldsmith College, March 4.

Glazer, Nathan, and Daniel P. Moynihan. 1963. *Beyond the Melting Pot*. Cambridge, Mass: MIT Press.

Gmelch, G. 1992. *Double Passage: The Lives of Caribbean Migrants Abroad and Back Home*. Ann Arbor: University of Michigan Press.

Goldman, Abigail. 1997. "For Latinos, Contacts Key to Getting Jobs." *San Francisco Examiner*, November 30, p. C7.

Gonzalez, G., and V. Breen. 1998. "Rain Dampens Day Only Slightly." *New York Daily News*, September 8, p. 7.

Gordon, M. 1983. *The Selection of Migrant Categories from the Caribbean to the United States: The Jamaican Experience*. New York: Center for Caribbean Studies.

Hall, S. 1990. "Cultural Identity and Diaspora." In *Identity, Community, Culture, Difference*, ed. Jonathan Rutherford. London: Lawrence and Wishart.

———. 1995. "Negotiating Caribbean Identities." *New Left Review* 209 (January–February): 3–14.

Henke, H. 2001. *The West Indian Americans.* Westport, Conn.: Greenwood Press.

Hernandez-Reguant, Ariana. 2000. "Kwanzaa and the U.S. Ethnic Mosaic." In *Representations of Blackness,* ed. John Muteba Rahier, pp. 101–22. Westport, Conn.: Bergen and Garvey.

Hill, Donald R. 1994. "West Indian Carnival in New York." *New York Folklore* 20, nos. 1 and 2: 47–66.

Hintzen, Percy C. 1999. "Identity, Arena, and Performance: Being West Indian in the San Francisco Bay Area." In *Representations of Blackness and the Performance of Identities,* ed. John Muteba Rahier, pp. 123–46. Westport, Conn.: Bergen and Garvey.

Ho, C. 1991. *Salt-Water Trinnies: Afro-Trinidadian Immigrant Networks and Non-Assimilation in Los Angeles.* New York: AMS Press.

Horne, Gerald. 1995. *Fire This Time: The Watts Uprising and the 1960s.* Charlottesville: University Press of Virginia.

James, W. 1998. *Holding Aloft the Banner of Ethiopia: Caribbean Radicalism in Early Twentieth-Century America.* London: Verso.

Justus, Joyce B. 1983. "West Indians in Los Angeles: Community and Identity." In *Caribbean Immigration to the United States.* 2d ed., ed. Roy S. Bryce-Laporte and Delores M. Mortimer, pp. 130–48. Washington, D.C.: Smithsonian Institution, Research Institute on Immigration and Ethnic Studies.

Kasinitz, Phillip. 1992. *Caribbean New York: Black Immigrants and the Politics of Race.* Ithaca, N.Y.: Cornell University Press.

———. 1988. "From Ghetto Elite to Service Sector: A Comparison of Two Waves of West Indian Immigrants in New York City." *Ethnic Groups* 7: 173–204.

Levine, B. B. 1987. *The Caribbean Exodus.* New York: Praeger.

Lieberson, S., and Mary C. Waters. 1990. *From Many Strands.* New York: Russell Sage Foundation.

Manning, Frank. 1990. "Overseas Caribbean Carnivals: The Arts and Politics of a Transnational Celebration. In *Caribbean Poplar Culture,* ed. J. Lent, pp. 20–36. Bowling Green, Ohio: Bowling Green University Popular Press.

Marable, Manning, ed. 1980. *From the Grassroots.* Boston: South End Press.

Mission Economic and Cultural Association. 1994. Press release, April 22.

Model, S. 1991. "Caribbean Immigrants: A Black Success Story?" *International Migration Review* 25 (Summer): 249–75.

———. 1995. "West Indian Prosperity: Fact or Fiction?" *Social Problems* 42, no. 4 (November): 535–52.

Moore, Colin. 1985. "Some Reflections on Labor Day Carnival." *New York Carib News* 24 (September): 15.

Nettleford, Rex. 1988. "The Implications of Caribbean Development." In

Caribbean Festival Arts, ed. John Nunley and Judith Bettleheim, pp. 183–97. Seattle: University of Washington Press.

Noel, Peter. 1994a. "All Dat Is Mas: Understanding the West Indian Carnival." *New York Times*, September 6, p. 33.

———. 1994b. "The Politics of Carnival: Raining on the West Indian Parade." *Village Voice*, September 6, p. 30.

Noguera-Devers, Aurora. 1991. "The Factors Responsible for the Economic Success of West Indian Migrants." Senior thesis, University of California at Berkeley.

Nunley, John, and Judith Bettelheim, eds. 1988. *Caribbean Festival Arts*. Seattle: University of Washington Press.

Nurse, Keith. 1999. "Globalization and Trinidad Carnival: Diaspora, Hybridity and Identity in Global Culture." *Cultural Studies* 13, no. 4: 661–90.

Office of the Mayor of New York. 1997. Press release 049-97. January 28.

Oliver, Melvin. 1994. Blacks Aren't Hogging Postal Service Jobs." *Los Angeles Times*, August 12, p. B7.

Palmer, R. 1990. *In Search of a Better Life: Perspectives on Migration from the Caribbean*. New York: Praeger.

Petersen, William. 1971. *Japanese Americans: Oppression and Success*. New York: Random House.

Pierre-Pierre, G. 1993. "West Indians Adding Clout at Ballot Box." *New York Times*, September 6, p. B1.

Portes. A. 1994. "Caribbean Diasporas: Migration and Ethnic Communities." *Annals of the American Academy of Political and Social Science* 533 (May): 48–69.

Purdy, Matthew. 1991. "In Brooklyn, Steel Drums and a Truce." *New York Times*, September 3, p. B1.

———. 1994. "Parade Shows off West Indian Political Clout." *New York Times*, September 6, p. 1.

Rand California. 2000. "Housing Prices and Transaction Statistics." June 15. [Internet]

Raphael, L. 1964. "West Indians and Afro-Americans." *Freedomways*, Summer, pp. 438–45.

Rex, John. 1982. "West Indian and Asian Youth." In *Black Youth in Crisis*, ed. E. Cashmore and Barry Troyna, eds., pp. 53–71. London: Allen & Unwin.

Richardson, B. C. 1983. *Caribbean Migrants*. Knoxville: University of Tennessee Press.

Roberts, S. 1994. "In Middle-Class Queens, Blacks Pass Whites in Household Income." *New York Times*, June 6, p. A1.

San Jose Mercury News. 2000. "The Cost of Living in Silicon Valley." Special report. June 15. [*Mercury News* homepage]

Sassen-Koob, S. 1981. "Exporting Capital and Importing Labor: The Role of

Caribbean Migration to New York City." Occasional Papers of New York Research Program in Inter-American Affairs, no. 28. New York: New York University.

Saverino, Joan.1996. "Italians in Public Memory: Pageantry, Power, and Imagining the Italian American, 1923–1940." Balch Faculty Forum 1998–99. Philadelphia: Balch Institute for Ethnic Studies.

Sengupta, Somini, and Gary Pierre-Pierre. 1998. "A Tradition Remade in Brooklyn: West Indians Prepare a Lavish, and Popular, Pageant." *New York Times*, September 5, p. B1.

Solomon, Patrick R. 1992. *Black Resistance in School: Forging a Separatist Culture*. Albany: State University of New York Press.

Sonenshein, Raphael. 1993. *Politics in Black and White: Race and Power in Los Angeles*. Princeton, N.J.: Princeton University Press.

Sowell, Thomas. 1978. "Three Black Histories." In *American Ethnic Groups*, ed. Thomas Sowell and Lynn D. Collins, pp. 37–64. Washington, D.C.: Urban Institute.

Stannard, Matthew. 2001. "East Palo Alto Back from the Brink." *San Francisco Chronicle*, January 2, pp. A1, A6.

Steinberg, Stephen. 1981. *The Ethnic Myth: Race, Class and Ethnicity in America*. Boston: Beacon Press.

Strozier, Matthew. 1997. "West Indian Day Parade; Indo-Caribbeans Play Minor Role." *India in New York*, September 5. [India in New York homepage]

Sutton, C., and E. M. Chaney, eds. 1987. *Caribbean Life in New York City: Sociocultural Dimensions*. New York: Center for Migration Studies.

Tidrick, K. 1971. "Need for Achievement, Social Class, and Intention to Emigrate in Jamaican Students." *Social and Economic Studies* 20, no. 1 (March): 52–60.

U.S. Bureau of the Census. 1991. *1990 Census of Population*. Washington, D.C.: U.S. Government Printing Office.

U.S. Department of Housing and Urban Development 2000. "Estimated Median Family Incomes for Fiscal Year 2000." PDR-00-01. March 9. [Internet homepage]

U.S. Immigration and Naturalization Service. 1984. *Statistical Yearbook 1980*. Washington, D.C.: U.S. Government Printing Office.

Vickerman, M. 1994. "The Response of West Indians towards African-Americans: Distancing and Identification." In *Research in Race and Ethnic Relations*, vol. 7, ed. Dennis Routledge, pp. 83–128. Greenwich, Conn.: JAI Press.

———. 1999. *Crosscurrents: West Indian Immigration and Race*. New York: Oxford University Press.

Wagner, Venise. 2000. "Blacks Losing Clout in S.F." *San Francisco Examiner*, October 29, pp. A-1, A-14.

Waldinger, R. 1987. "The Jobs Immigrants Take." *New York Times*, March 1, p. A17.

———. 1996. *Still the Promised City?: African Americans and New Immigrants in Post Industrial New York*. Cambridge, Mass.: Harvard University Press.

Walt, V. 1988. "Caught between Two Worlds: Immigrants Discover Success, Racism in the U.S." *New York Newsday*, April 15, pp. 9–27.

Waters, Mary C. 1990. *Ethnic Options*. Berkeley and Los Angeles: University of California Press.

———. 1994. "Ethnic and Racial Identities of Second Generation Black Immigrants in New York City." *International Migration Review* 28: 785–820.

Watkins, O. I. 1996. *Blood Relations: Caribbean Immigrants and the Harlem Community, 1900–1930*. Bloomington: Indiana University Press.

Woldemikel, T. M. 1989. *Becoming Black American: Haitians and American Institutions in Evanston, Illinois*. New York: AMS Press.

Wired homepage [Internet]. 1999. "Up with the Valley." Feature archive 7.07, July.

Wyman, Bill. 1987. "Roots: The Origins of Black Politics in the East Bay." *Express* 9, no. 43 (August 7).

Yelvington, K. A. 1995 . *Producing Power: Ethnicity, Gender, and Class in a Caribbean Workplace*. Philadelphia: Temple University Press.

Yong-Jin, Wong. 1994. "'Model Minority' Strategy and Asian American Tactics." *Korea Journal*, Summer, pp. 57–66.

Index

About the Author

Percy C. Hintzen is an associate professor, the chair of African American studies, and the former director of peace and conflict studies at the University of California at Berkeley. He is the author of *The Costs of Regime Survival: Racial Mobilization, Elite Domination, and Control of the State in Guyana and Trinidad.*